G80204091

SHAW IN HIS TIME

G.B.S. at home

Shaw
IN HIS TIME

IVOR BROWN

NELSON

THOMAS NELSON AND SONS LTD
36 Park Street London W1
Parkside Works Edinburgh 9
P.O. Box 336 Apapa Lagos
P.O. Box 25012 Nairobi

THOMAS NELSON (AUSTRALIA) LTD
597 Little Collins Street Melbourne

THOMAS NELSON & SONS (SOUTH AFRICA) (PROPRIETARY) LTD
P.O. Box 9881 Johannesburg

THOMAS NELSON AND SONS (CANADA) LTD
81 Curlew Drive Don Mills Ontario

THOMAS NELSON AND SONS
Copewood and Davis Streets Camden 3, N.J.

First published in Great Britain by Thomas Nelson and Sons Ltd 1965

Made and printed in Great Britain by
Thomas Nelson (Printers) Ltd, Edinburgh, for
Thomas Nelson and Sons Ltd, 36 Park Street, London, W.1

CONTENTS

ILLUSTRATIONS

ACKNOWLEDGMENTS

The author and publishers wish to thank the Public Trustee and the Society of Authors for permission to use extracts from Shaw's writings and correspondence, and Mr Laurence Irving for permission to quote from his book, *Henry Irving*.

CHAPTER ONE

Shaw's Ireland

G EORGE BERNARD SHAW was born in Dublin on July 26th, 1856.
He was married in London on June 1st, 1898, to Charlotte
Townsend, who was born at Derry in County Cork on January 20th,
1857. The father of G.B.S., George Carr Shaw, was a civil servant
who in later life capitalized his small pension to buy himself a partnership in a milling business. He was a kind-hearted muddler with small
capacity for such affairs and took to bouts of heavy drinking; naturally the venture was a failure. Fortunately his wife was an able
musician and could earn money by giving singing lessons. It was a
poor home but not an unhappy one. Despite poverty and insecurity,
there was pride in a middle-class status. 'I was born in a house,' wrote
Shaw in one of his latest books, *Sixteen Self-Sketches,* 'where there
was a kitchen and a drawing-room and always at least one "thorough-
servant", paid eight pounds a year in cash and lodged in the basement.'
A 'thorough-servant' was presumably the person called 'a general' in
England and a maid of all work.

Charlotte Townsend of Derry belonged to a county family whose
prosperity grew because of her father's shrewd methods of investment. She was brought up in comfort and well educated by an able
governess. Thus Shaw, who began his wage-earning life as junior
clerk in an estate agency, filing letters and taking impressions of them
in a copying-press at a salary of eighteen pounds a year, may be said
to have married above his station. But by the time of his wedding he
was a professional man of letters with a rapidly increasing reputation
for novelty of ideas and brilliance of style. Since at her parents' death
Charlotte inherited enough to be called an heiress, it was suggested

*Shaw's birthplace,
33 Synge Street,
Dublin*

by the malicious that Shaw married for money. But this is untrue. By 1898 he had escaped from the long penury of his early years in London and had made a name as dramatic critic and dramatist; he was earning sufficient to be independent of his wife's private income.

Before she became Mrs Shaw, Charlotte had become Miss Payne-Townshend. Her snobbish English mother, formerly a Miss Kirby, had thought some social advancement could be made by inserting the letter 'h' into Townsend. As the 'h' was not pronounced the insistence on it seems doubly ridiculous. She had also demanded the introduction of the hyphenated Payne, which was a family name on her side. Her husband did not like this fussy change, but he was constantly over-ridden by a determined and dominating wife. Charlotte had no interest in such nonsense; she sympathised continually with her much-vexed father who wanted to stay on his Irish estate and resented being dragged to the social gaieties of Dublin and London and the foreign travel in which his gadabout wife delighted. In time Charlotte had more than sympathy for her father who much preferred the tranquillity of a country life. She was so angered by the domestic nagging and tyranny that she came actually to hate her

mother; her life in an unhappy home produced a neurotic repulsion
from the very idea of marriage; she thought of it as a form of union
which she could not endure and would not enter.

So with a shabby-genteel home in Dublin on one side and the
wealthy, well-staffed country house of Derry on the other, the Shaws
represented two contrasting Irelands in the second half of the nineteenth century. Yet we do not encounter the essential Ireland in
either household since the occupants of both were Protestants and
thus separated by a rigid bar from the great majority of the people
who, except in the north-eastern region of Ulster, were hereditary
and devoted Catholics. In general the owners of land and property
were members of the Protestant Episcopal Church of Ireland; this
Anglican body was so named by Shaw with reference to his baptism
therein. The peasants and urban proletarians held firmly to their
traditional Roman faith.

To generalize about 'the Irish' is a common but futile occupation.
Islands attract mixed populations if they are worth over-running by
force, and there had been a plentiful mixture of blood in the frequently
invaded and commercially infiltrated Ireland. The most drastic seizure of its land followed Cromwell's expeditionary force, some of
whose members remained as an alien class of owners and settlers,
English over-lords among the aboriginal Gaels. From these came the
Anglo-Irish land-owners scattered about the country and above the
people. They took the best land and then rented it, or rack-rented it,
to the natives, whose territory, if they kept any of their own, was
remote and rocky land, incapable of easy and profitable farming.

Ireland has copious rain and a central bowl of soil good for pasture,
but on its mountainous rim the earth lies thin upon the stone; cultivation was a back-breaking and heart-breaking occupation for those
driven out of the central fertility. I remember that, while I was staying in the far West just before the rebellion of 1920, which turned
John Bull's Other Island into the Free State and finally the Republic
of Eire, I asked why the fields were so small and the walls so many
and so high. It was pointed out to me that there would be no fields

at all unless the people had dug up the stones with hand-labour and piled them up in these frequent and formidable dikes. Yet such was the land-hunger that the small farmers were quarrelling violently over a disputed yard or two and would even use shot-guns to settle the argument. The soil thus uncovered by delving was so thin as to yield but a miserable living if the tenants had paid no rent at all. While the land was infertile, the men and women were not. Poverty and over-population are constant companions all over the world. Ireland was teeming with large families and emigration was the only remedy for over-crowding in the congested areas. Methods of birth control were unknown and the priests were determined that such knowledge should never be allowed to come in.

In the North East there was a plantation of Scots, Protestant to the core, many of them urban workers in and around Belfast and all bristling at the name of Rome. To speak of a Mayo farmer and an industrial employer or worker in Ulster both as Irish makes sense only in a geographical way. In addition to these elements there had been a small incursion of Spanish in Connemara on the western coast. Its principal town, Galway, was a major harbour in the days of sail and a valuable link with the European and especially the Spanish trade, thus bringing foreign settlers. That prosperity dwindled away; so did later hopes of Galway's becoming an important port of call for transatlantic steam-ships. The great stone warehouses of the old merchants remained as gaunt ruins in what had once been an important and flourishing city.

Here, as elsewhere and especially on the eastern side of Ireland, there had been the influx of milords from England, fond of hunting and fishing and sometimes seeking methods of improving agriculture and developing rural industry. There was also a steady growth of the Anglo-Irish and Protestant middle-class who had neither race nor religion in common with the natives from whom they were glad to be protected by military forces and a special police force called the Royal Irish Constabulary. Many of these prospered in their professional occupations or the forms of commerce large enough to be

4

deemed socially respectable, while others, like Shaw's father, could not settle to a career and failed to thrive. But rich or poor they kept themselves to themselves. They had their own schools, Protestant, of course, and would not have their children rubbing shoulders with the young Papists whose parents were shopkeepers or manual workers. A popular song has long celebrated the smile in Irish eyes; but there was little hilarity and much hatred in the island where Shaw was born.

The Protestant and fairly prosperous minority were known as the Ascendancy. The members of that class included the country squires of whom Horace Townsend, Charlotte's father, was a creditable example. He was a good type of Anglo-Irish gentleman. While accepting 'the rich man in his castle, the poor man at his gate' as a divine dispensation, a view conveniently held by most of his class, he was ready to do his best for the peasants and to forward any local schemes likely to increase the resources of a desperately poor people. There were others far less considerate who drew all the rents they could wring from their people and spent them on sport at home or in a pleasure-seeking life in London.

The Catholic peasantry of mid-Victorian Ireland had bitter memories of past history and bitter experience of present miseries. The conquest which Queen Elizabeth's expeditionary forces had failed to make the Ironsides had brutally achieved. During the eighteenth century the Irish were still being victimised for their support of the Stuarts; the English had been strong enough to enforce repressive and tyrannical laws. The Irish farmer could not own land and he had to pay tithes for the support of the Anglican clergy whose churches he did not attend and which had tiny con-gregations. While an alien Church was thus endowed the priests of the native and Roman faith had to be supported by contributions from the peasants. Catholics, however well qualified, could not hold official positions until the Emancipation Act of 1829.

.It seems astonishing that this domination known as the Ascendancy was endured for so long. But it had its army and its police. It was in

fact a garrison as well as a commercial and proprietorial settlement.
In the capital it ruled, or mis-ruled, from Dublin Castle. Prominent
features in the countryside were the barracks and the gaol. Thus the
Ascendancy was powerful enough to survive all discontent until it
was defeated in the nineteen-twenties when violent insurrection at
last achieved what votes could not. The peasants of Victorian Ireland
were unorganized and no match for well-fed and well-trained
opponents.

What could be earned by rearing pigs and poultry had to be set
aside to pay the rent. Evictions often followed failure to pay. The
national staple in the countryside was the potato. If that crop failed
there was starvation; and it did disastrously fail ten years before the
birth of Shaw and Charlotte when famine killed many thousands
and increased emigration of the survivors to America on a gigantic
scale. The best thing that an Irish peasant could hope for in the
eighteen-forties was to get out of Ireland. Some desperate men

Irish emigrants leaving home

known as Moonlighters fought the Ascendancy by arson, nocturnal raiding, and maiming of cattle. The Fenians, named after Feinne, a legendary band of heroes, were actively insurgent in England as well as Ireland. But the Garrison held its ground. The brew of hatred had to ferment for many years before it could be so strengthened and inspirited as to press home by guerilla warfare a finally triumphant rebellion.

Yet it would be wrong to think of the Ascendancy families as all composed of selfish and predatory malefactors. Invaders they were, but they included competent settlers who could manage their property in a capable way. From them too came some people of remarkable character who were moved, even fired, by an eager devotion to Irish causes. A notable example of this was Augusta Persse (1852–1932) who became Lady Gregory of Coole in Galway and the friend and frequent hostess of W. B. Yeats. Elizabeth Coxhead in her life of Lady Gregory related that the Persses were a branch of the Percys of Northumberland who came to Ireland in Cromwellian times. They prospered and multiplied. As was perhaps natural to the house of Hotspur some became distinguished soldiers in the British army. Others remained farming squires 'with an aptitude for getting hold of the best grazing land and making it pay'. Some of the Persses were accused of harshness to tenants, others of seeking to convert Roman Catholics to Protestantism, a practice much resented by the native Irish and their priests. There could be no charges of inhumanity or religious interference against Augusta despite her loyalty to the Protestant Episcopal Church of Ireland.

She was brought up on the big, well-run Persse estate of Roxborough and gave it dutiful service. Instead of thinking of the social whirl at the Viceroy's receptions in Dublin, a principal centre of Ascendancy junketing, or yielding to the lure of a fashionable London season, much enjoyed by the wealthy Anglo-Irish daughters, she remained a social worker among her own people. Thus she became fascinated by the primitive Ireland of the peasants and especially by the Gaelic legends. These she translated as narratives

7

which became praised and popular in England and America. She also used the myths and sagas as themes for plays. When she married Sir William Gregory and long survived him as the owner of Coole, she became more and more determined that Ireland should have its new voice in poetry and drama, not only recreating the old stories of the mythical heroes but presenting to the world the humours and sufferings of the country-folk in her own time and place. The Irish literary and dramatic renaissance which came at the end of the nineteenth century owed much to the Anglo-Irish of the Ascendancy class.

That is not surprising since illiteracy was widespread in the country and also among the poorer workers in the cities. The priests were powerful and were not as a rule interested in the arts or education except of a narrow kind. If the people's voice was to be heard in books and plays, few of them could speak for themselves. Later on Sean O'Casey was a notable exception, but he owed his first theatrical opportunities to Dublin's Abbey Theatre which was founded in 1904. It would not have been there at all without the financial backing of the English Miss Horniman and the enthusiastic labours of Lady Gregory and W. B. Yeats, who both came from Ascendancy families. Yeats's grandfather always floated the Union Jack on the flag-staff outside his house in Sligo and in his boyhood the poet had fancied that his finest hour would be fighting the Fenians to the death. Shaw, on the other hand, declared himself 'a boyhood Fenian'.

The life of a girl in County Cork society is vividly drawn in the fascinating biography of Charlotte Townsend by Janet Dunbar entitled *Mrs. G.B.S.* There were easy relations with the people on the estate because Horace Townsend was, as long as his wife permitted, a benevolent resident and not ashamed of being Irish. For young people there was plenty of dancing, riding, and hunting with young men of their class and officers of the English garrison. The Ascendancy families used to visit each other for leisurely stays in the big houses. The Townsends were unlikely to be special targets of the actively rebellious minority; the Catholic priests who had great

8

authority over their community could not encourage violence and wanted a quiet life. Nationalist politics without Fenian ferocity satisfied them. They were much concerned with the chastity of the young people. In Southern Ireland the Roman Church was and has long remained puritanical in its discipline; a fraction of the exposure of feminine flesh which is taken for granted today would have been regarded as sinful in the extreme. In Shaw's play *John Bull's Other Island* the girl Nora is outraged by the clumsy but innocent approaches of the emotional Englishman Broadbent. The broader views of European Catholicism were taboo in the island of St Patrick, where the doctrine came from Rome and the moral code was as rigid as among English Chapel-folk.

The Shaws in Dublin were not all Somebodies on the way to becoming Nobodies, as G.B.S. described his family. They still possessed and were proud of their links with the land-owning class which had its reckless and dissipated members eager to mortgage their property when they ran into trouble. A second cousin of George Carr Shaw was a baronet, Sir Robert Shaw of Bushey Park, Terenure. But other branches of the family had drifted down to the lower fringe of the Ascendancy. When Shaw was called an upstart later in life he retorted that he came from a family of down-starts. But his kindred were genteel despite their poverty and rigidly Protestant.

The word Protestant acquired a negative sense in Ireland. It primarily meant 'not a Roman'. What was believed was much less important than what was disbelieved, especially with regard to the great enemy, Rome. To be 'Prot' was a social safeguard; it did not necessitate piety and regular church-going. The father of G.B.S. was no pillar of the church. His son found him humane and humorous as well as an alcoholic. Religion was not a subject for hushed and solemn mention in the home. Shaw recorded in the eighth of his *Self-Sketches* his opinion that, as far as the Protestant gentry were concerned, Ireland was the most irreligious country in the world.

He himself was duly christened but his appointed godfather was drunk at the appointed hour and did not appear; so the sexton acted as understudy. Thus oddly introduced to the Protestant Church he was never confirmed in it. He believed that his parents also remained in that state of no grace. Irish Protestantism, he wrote, 'was not a religion, but a side in a political faction, a class prejudice, a conviction that Roman Catholics are socially inferior persons who will go to hell when they die and leave Heaven in the exclusive possession of Protestant ladies and gentlemen.' He noticed that the Protestant clergy did not want any poor parishioners of the working-class in their congregations; poverty and Papism went together and both were deemed disreputable.

Shaw's maternal uncle, Walter Gurley, went to Trinity College, one of the Ascendancy strongholds, and became a doctor. He combined the formal religion of his youth with Rabelaisian humour and was a gay blasphemer. As a small boy G.B.S. was made to put in routine appearances at a Sunday school; that has always been a convenient method of getting the children out of the way when the parents want a Sunday sleep. But his father was quite ready to jest about sacred matters and, when asked by his son what the Unitarians were, he replied with a laugh that these people believed that Jesus was not successfully crucified by the Roman soldiers but was seen running down the other side of the Hill of Calvary. 'This,' said Shaw, 'I believed for thirty years.'

The boy was sent for education to the Wesleyan Connexional School which was of course strictly Protestant. There he learned very little, and later, on the advice of his mother's music-teacher, Vandeleur Lee, he was moved for better instruction to the Central Model Boys' School. This was supposed to be undenominational and classless, but was in fact a nest of Roman Catholics. By going within these gates he knew that he was losing caste. As he put it: 'That the son of a Protestant merchant-gentleman and feudal downstart should pass those bars and associate in any way with its hosts of lower middle-class Catholic children, sons of petty shopkeepers and tradesmen, was inconceivable from the Shaw point of view.'

G.B.S. compared his attendance at this socially discreditable school to the sufferings and humiliations of Charles Dickens in the blacking factory. Dickens felt that he had been wounded for life by his mother's consent to that drudgery when he should have been at school. Shaw in the *Self-Sketch* called *Shame and Wounded Snobbery* confessed that he felt that a similar enduring insult and injustice had been imposed on him by his Catholic contacts and not until the end of his life could he bear to mention this episode in his education. The infamy had to be pushed out of mind and stayed thus buried until he found relief for a guilty conscience by admitting his boyish folly.

Trinity College in Dublin had a fine tradition of scholarship, but that was beyond the range of George Carr Shaw's purse and his ambitions for his son. The boy's schooling was of a mixed and mediocre kind, but at least it left him free from over-education. He was not crammed to pass examinations, driven to work for a university scholarship, and then set to one of the various courses which would win a degree. For youngsters with no intellectual appetite and a boorish home this freedom from curriculum disciplines provided a pleasant opportunity to remain ignorant. But G.B.S. made the absence of academic pressures the chance to get what self-education he could find. Long attendance at school and university might, in the unlikely event of his enduring it to the end, have cramped his mind while filling it. Thus a bad education was really a good one for a youngster with initiative and a readiness to go about and learn what he could where he could. Shaw found ample scope for abundant self-teaching through the enjoyment of books and music at home and of the graphic arts in the National Picture Gallery which he frequented. By his own account he had it very much to himself and also, by his account, he was far from being under-educated.

The city had its theatres and there was sufficient support for the drama to attract English companies of quality. Thus Shaw had his juvenile and very favourable impression of Henry Irving who visited

Dublin as a member of the London company, playing the part of Digby Grant in Albery's popular piece *The Two Roses*. Shaw was struck by the unusual quality of this magnetic presence and by a performance which stood out vividly from the rest. 'I felt,' he wrote later, 'that a new drama inhered in this man, though I had then no conscious notion that I was destined to write it.' That Irving would not commit himself to the Shavian innovations when written stimulated Shaw's critical attacks on Irving's theatrical policy; of this more will be said later.

One of the major pleasures of Shaw's early play-going lay in the appearances of an Irish actor, Barry Sullivan, a powerful Shakespearian actor from Cork who had some success in many parts of the world. From the accounts of his work it seems that he would now be dismissed as 'ham', but Shaw, not yet a vegetarian at the table, was evidently ready for Sullivan's red meat in the theatre. It was said that Sullivan's rough style and visage scarred by smallpox unfitted him for romantic parts, but he did so well and was so much liked when he played the part of Hamlet at the Haymarket Theatre in London that he was taken on by Samuel Phelps for a season at Sadlers Wells; he was later chosen for the first male leading part when the Shakespeare Memorial Theatre was opened at Stratford-upon-Avon in 1879. He then played Benedick to Helen Faucit's Beatrice; the role needs a personal attraction. At any rate he attracted Shaw to Shakespeare in the theatre; of Shakespeare in print he had been an addict since the age of ten.

Victorian Dublin had melodrama in plenty supplied by Dionysius, better known as Dion, Boucicault. He was of Irish extraction and he wrote skilfully to satisfy Irish sentiment in *The Colleen Bawn, The Shaughraun* and other pieces which remained favourites for half a century. His power of invention and skill in construction were those of a master-craftsman in the popular dramas of romance, daring, self-sacrifice, and love triumphant. Another theme to delight Dublin audiences not of the Ascendancy class was the drama of native insurrection in which the English appeared as villainous oppressors.

These were still on view long after the Abbey had become the National Theatre of Ireland and the national spirit was made manifest in the audience by the lusty cheering of the Irish patriots on the stage and the hisses and boos which greeted the appearance of the red-coats. While the Ascendancy folk were numerous enough to attract good English companies to make Irish visits, the bulk of the urban population liked its music-hall and its melodrama, which could be combined with pints of porter and a sedentary, non-violent, and safe enough defiance of the alien overlords. During the Irish tour already mentioned, I went to the Abbey Theatre to see Shaw's play *The Devil's Disciple*. Even then the audience cheered lustily at a reference to 'a pig-headed lunatic like King George'. George III or George V, it was a chance to deride.

A native Irish theatre with serious intentions was not thought of until more than twenty years after Shaw's departure from Dublin. There had long been a Society for the Preservation of the Irish Language, but this had no popular roots. The language question did not excite the nationalist politicians and the Roman Church made no conspicuous efforts to sustain the native speech of the Gael. The British government kept it out of the schools. But the formation of the Gaelic League in 1893 did rouse more interest owing to the work put into it by some active enthusiasts. Chief among these was Douglas Hyde, an organizer as well as a poet and dramatist, who published his *Love Songs of Connacht* in the original Irish with an English translation, a volume which had considerable influence.

Standish O'Grady was another early champion of Gaelic culture, especially in its tale-telling of the bards and in the sagas of the ancient heroes. Edward Martyn, a Catholic land-owner with cultural interests, had the idea of writing plays in Irish, obviously with insufficient understanding of the number of playgoers likely to understand them. Meanwhile London was doing in a small way what Dublin was not doing at all. J. T. Grein's Independent Theatre, which introduced both Ibsen and Shaw to London audiences, albeit very small ones, produced Yeats's *Land of Heart's Desire* at the Avenue Theatre in

1894. Here was Ireland's voice in excellent English, not what the zealots of the Gaelic League wanted, but a reminder that Ireland could earn a place in the internationalism of Grein's theatrical plans and programme.

A scheme for what was called the Irish Literary Theatre was formulated in 1898 with Lady Gregory as an enthusiastic supporter and Edward Martyn as a financial benefactor. Its manifesto declared a hopeful belief in 'an uncorrupted and imaginative Irish audience'. The purpose was to bring upon the stage 'the deeper thoughts and emotions of Ireland' and to show that 'Ireland is not the home of buffoonery and easy sentiment, as it has been represented, but the home of an ancient idealism'. The big Dublin theatres were not within reach of the modest funds available; so the first performance was given in May, 1899, at the ancient Concert Rooms in Great Brunswick Street; the plays offered, of course in English, were Martyn's *The Heather Field* and Yeats's *The Countess Cathleen*.

The Irish audience were infuriated by Yeats's piece and demonstrated their disgust with rowdiness. *The Countess Cathleen* was said to be anti-Irish and anti-Catholic. Catholic students from University College made so much trouble that the Irish Literary Theatre had to begin its life with police protection, a bitterly ironic happening since the police were regarded as the minions of British tyranny. Of course the charges against Yeats were nonsensical. The idealists of the Literary Theatre had received a rough answer to their belief in 'an uncorrupted and imaginative Irish audience'. But it could be said that the uproarious protesters, however obtuse, were taking the theatre seriously.

During the next two years the Literary Theatre imported English companies to act Irish plays, one of which was written by George Moore. Then came a most important step, the formation of a company of Irish players with Frank and William Fay to lead and direct them. In 1903 it presented plays by Yeats, Lady Gregory, Padraic Colum, and J. M. Synge. The performances were so well received that a visit to London was made and there the critical appreciation

Lady Gregory

was most encouraging. It evoked what was more valuable at the time than favourable verdicts in print. That was the backing of Miss Horniman, whose cheque-book made the Abbey Theatre possible.

She was English and of Quaker stock, as far removed as might be from the religion of the Irish people and the background of the new Irish play-writing. But her contribution gave the Literary Theatre its chance to become something much larger and more enduring. 'Curious,' wrote A. E. Marlowe in his history of *The Irish Drama,* 'that in this stream of causes the practical persons should be women and the dreamers men. To Lady Gregory first and to Miss Horniman in only slightly lesser degree must go the credit for the Irish Theatre.' Lady Gregory was subsequently derided by some who thought that a woman who continued to wear widow's weeds with the prolonged fidelity to mourning of a Queen Victoria must be inconsiderable in the sphere of the arts. But she was a woman of resolve and became the force behind the writers while rising in capacity as a dramatist, especially successful in her short plays.

Shaw was away from all this. By the end of the century he was fully engaged as a playwright in London with a growing public all over the world. In the Preface to *John Bull's Other Island,* which was written in 1904, he asserted and defined his sense of nationality.

'When I say that I am an Irishman I mean that I was born in Ireland, and that my native language is the English of Swift and not the unspeakable jargon of the mid-XIX century London newspapers. My extraction is the extraction of most Englishmen: that is, I have no trace in me of the commercially imported North Spanish strain which passes for aboriginal Irish: I am a genuine typical Irishman of the Danish, Norman, Cromwellian, and (of course) Scotch invasions. I am violently and arrogantly Protestant by family tradition; but let no English Government therefore count on my allegiance: I am English enough to be an inveterate Republican and Home Ruler.'

The play thus introduced was written on the request of Yeats 'as a patriotic contribution to the Irish Literary Theatre'. Its production was thought to be too large an undertaking for the newly founded Abbey Theatre; so it was passed over to the Vedrenne-Barker management at the Court Theatre in London where Shaw's plays were being presented and kept in its repertory. It won considerable success and was greatly appreciated not only by the increasing number of loyal Shavians but by some of the statesmen of the time. Arthur Balfour, the Conservative Prime Minister, took the leaders of the Liberal opposition, Campbell-Bannerman and Asquith, to see it on more than one occasion. It was even commanded and enjoyed by Edward VII, who had been more annoyed than amused by *Arms and the Man*. It is curious that it has dropped out of the list of Shaw's plays that are frequently revived. The fact that the independence of Southern Ireland has long been achieved does not lessen its value as a period piece and the commentary on English and Irish character, which is the most important element of the comedy, is by no means out-of-date.

16

Shaw, though he several times wrote of past ages and persons, was chiefly concerned with the present and the future. He had no sympathy with the preservation of a dwindling language and no interest in the saga heroes. He said that whenever he considered a theme which moved the Irish poets and the Gaelic Leaguers to lyrics and lamentations he found that he had to rationalize it and the result was comedy. In *John Bull's Other Island* he took his characters from the Ireland of the small farmers who, with no eye for seeing fairies, were realists about money and their lack of it. He was inconsistent, cursing the peasants for working too hard (for the benefit of the landlords) and then railing against the soft, relaxing climate which made them sleepy and created the Irish dreamer. Of this type he wrote, 'No debauchery that ever coarsened and brutalized an Englishman can take the usefulness out of him like dreaming. If you want to interest him in Ireland you have got to call the unfortunate island "Kathleen na Hoolihan" and pretend she is a little old woman.'

There was a dig at Yeats, who took it in good part and strongly approved of *John Bull's Other Island*. It was plain that Shaw could

W. B. Yeats

never work to the early pattern of the Irish Literary Theatre with its tendency to harp—and harp is here doubly the obvious word—on the old legends of Cuchulain and the often-sung sorrows of Deirdre. He could not be bothered with these children of the ancient mist; he had seen the children of the Dublin slums and the realities of Irish poverty, both urban and rural, in clear daylight. These seemed to him more urgent matters than the myths of the shadowy past. Lady Gregory liked questioning the old women round Coole about the fairies, apparently a numerous tribe, whom they saw in the woods. The 'little people' were less attractive to Shaw than human beings. His *John Bull's Other Island* has a visionary priest, it is true, but the Irish characters are otherwise concerned with pigs, acres, and rentals. The elves do not appear.

Shaw was a nationalist in the expulsive sense; he wanted the British government to pack up and go. He himself packed up and went at the age of twenty and did not revisit the country for nearly thirty years. During that time Parnell had raised Irish expectations of a parliamentary and peaceful victory for Home Rule. Parnell had gone, a personal tragedy, and Gladstone had split the Liberal party by his loyalty to the Irish cause; here was a political disaster for the Nationalists who saw the hated Union strengthened by the Liberal Unionists. The Irish members had to realize that, while able and angry voices were raised at Westminster, hopes were sadly lowered in their own country.

John Bull's other island remained in the hands of that owner and the Ulster corner of it was so doggedly Bullish that the prospect of an Ireland both self-governing and united became only another Irish dream. Further violence, including murder in Dublin's Phoenix Park, and a simmering peasant warfare in the West, was met with further repression. Concessions in the way of land reform did not appease. It was obvious to the rebels that John Bull would do anything for Ireland except get off its back and John was a heavy mount even if the animal under him were well-fed, which in this case it often was not. There was always hunger round the corner in the land of bog and rock and thousands every year continued to find the emigrants' ship more rewarding than the minor reforms achieved by agitation.

Nationalism to Shaw was a necessary evil, necessary because Home Rule was the only solution and such a concentration of political passion and energy on a single issue deflected attention from all other business. So, in his Preface to his Irish play, he cursed the island's nationalism as heartily as he did imperialism.

'Every election is fought on nationalist grounds; every appointment is made on nationalist grounds; every judge is a partisan in the nationalist conflict; every speech is a dreary recapitulation of nationalist twaddle; every lecture is a corruption of history to flatter nationalism or defame it; every school is a recruiting station; every church is a barrack; and every Irishman is unspeakably tired of the whole miserable business, which nevertheless is, and perforce must remain, his first business until Home Rule makes an end of it, and sweeps the nationalist and the garrison back together into the dustbin.'

So he was glad to be spending his formative years in London even though he had as slow a climb as any great writer ever endured to make an income and a name. Britain was tolerant of exiles who were malcontents or even determined revolutionists such as Marx and Lenin. Here, being free of an alien oppressor, the immigrants could begin their pioneering work for the overthrow of the ruling class. The English agitators, not afflicted by nationalism, did not have to waste their time on learning Anglo-Saxon to prove their English patriotism whereas the young Irish of radical views had to prove their nationalist loyalty and squander their time in learning, or failing to learn, the ancient language of the Gael.

Shaw left an Ireland that was so busy wearing the green that it had no time to think of buying a red tie. In any case, the Roman Church would have stopped any such move to the far Left in politics. Nationalism suited it well enough since it kept the young idea at home while Shaw, having the freedom of the British Museum Library with no censorship of the politics and philosophies he chose to read, could apply himself to European works on communism, atheism, and any other -ism in which his active and expanding mind delighted. If after the turn of the century the Irish Players brought their new drama to London he could listen to them undisturbed by the screams of the incensed Dublin Nationalists who thought that nothing should be said about Ireland that had not been licensed by patriots as ignorant of plays and poetry as they were incapable of civil behaviour.

Shaw's Preface already quoted contains abundant denunciation of the British, but he preferred residence in John Bull's own island to remaining in the other one, the land of his birth and breeding. For over seventy years he made his home in or near London and was never prosecuted for his opinions. His plays were occasionally banned by the Lord Chamberlain's censorship, but otherwise he enjoyed freedom of speech and writing and used that liberty to the full, hurling denunciations at the Britain which accepted and finally enriched him. In Ireland he would have been prosecuted and penniless. His preference for John Bull's bigger island was both reasonable and durable.

The Abbey Theatre as Shaw knew it

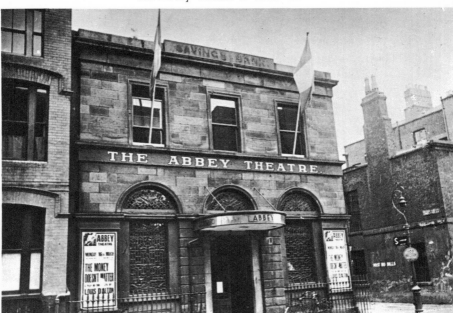

CHAPTER TWO

Shaw and the Theatre

IT is natural to wonder why Shaw made writing plays the greater part of his life-work. He constantly spoke of himself as a Puritan, not of course in the strict, sectarian, chapel-going sense, but as a man of serious purposes to whom politics and economics were a branch of morals, with the arts used to serve social ends. To the rigid Puritans, who once were many and powerful and now are few, the theatre had been, ever since it became popular and professional in Shakespeare's time, a source of corruption. But Shaw saw it as a means of correction. The Square Toes, as they had been called, thought miming and dressing-up a travesty of life and a denial of truth. Intellectual Puritanism of the Shavian kind held a creed altogether different. G. K. Chesterton, certainly as far from Puritanism in his faith as any man could be, was commendably fair to the Protestant, even the Protestant zealot at his best. In the first chapter of his book, *Bernard Shaw,* published in 1910, he wrote: 'Bernard Shaw exhibits all that is purest in the Puritan; the desire to see truth face to face even if it slay us, the high impatience with irrelevant sentiment or obstructive symbol; the constant effort to keep the soul at its highest pressure and speed. His instincts upon all social customs and questions are Puritan. His favourite author is Bunyan.' That is well said, but it does not answer the question why Shaw chose to seek the truth and proclaim it with Puritan thoroughness through a medium which one might have thought to be alien to his ascetic tastes and temperament.

One reason for that is the duality of the man. There were two Shaws. One was the prophet with doctrine in his head; the other

was the jester with a joke on his lips. He explained that, when he
began to preach, he found no listeners. So he did some mental
clowning in order to attract an audience. If he stood firmly with his
feet on the ground or the platform he had no audience. If he stood
with his head on the floor and his feet in the air the public thought
that he might deserve a laugh and even some attention. So, as a
devoted missioner, he was ready to be also the agile mountebank;
and he found that the trick worked.

That was his account of it, but the duality of the two roles was
really deeper than that. The actress who tried to conquer him, Mrs
Patrick Campbell, called him Joey, and not without cause. Shaw
enjoyed clowning as much as he enjoyed preaching. He was the
laughing cavalier of Socialism as well as its determined and diligent
advocate. His gospel of social salvation was stern. He could say hard
and cruel things, especially in the matter of capital punishment which
he did not oppose but recommended as a proper way of getting rid
of incorrigible idlers and social pests. But he made this plea on
humane grounds since he thought that long terms of imprisonment
were so devilishly cruel that a quick end was better than a life-long
torture. Shaw, as his friends and beneficiaries knew, was a most kind
and generous man in his private life. Why then should not a Puritan
of this genial type turn to a medium which the men of round heads
and square toes had so long regarded as Satanic? If using the actor's
stage was devilish to them, he, though as earnest a moralist as any,
was ready, in his own phrase, to be the devil's disciple.

In his early London life he had applied himself unsparingly to
Socialist propaganda. He learned the craft of the street-orator on the
pavement; he made long journeys to appear on platforms in small
and dismal halls where the audience might be tiny and the fee, as he
insisted, was always nothing. He was working in a bleak field. He
did not seek money; he sought believers. He practised with increasing mastery the art of pamphleteering and gave his time and skill in
that art to the Fabian Socialists. At that time he was beginning to
enjoy affairs with women but he boasted that he never missed a

platform engagement in order to keep a date with a lady. Life was real, life was earnest, and the theatre of his time was neither.

The hard facts of extreme poverty drove him to journalism which would somehow provide a pittance, and the journalism open to him was not of the political kind, since his views would have shocked and terrified all editors except those of Socialist sheets without a penny to spare when the printer had been paid. But he could write for a small but precious reward in survey of the arts without risking immediate dismissal, and among the arts was that of the theatre. Moreover, he had always liked the theatre and the easy-going Protestantism of his Dublin years did not forbid play going. One gets the feeling that all the time he had been that contradiction in terms, a stage-struck Puritan.

In his first playgoing he had despised the glamour of theatrical trappings and the romantic twaddle of the public's favourite plays. But none the less he must have quietly, almost secretly, enjoyed himself. And later, amid all the drudgery of Socialist propaganda, it occurred to him that the twaddle might possibly be replaced by the truth. Then, if the truth could be communicated with the warmth of the players' stage instead of with the austerity of the lecturer's dais, it would reach a large public who might come to be converted instead of a small one most of whom had come to applaud what they already believed. Chesterton's words, 'the constant effort to keep the soul at its highest pressure and speed', need amending in Shaw's case to pressure and speed of mind. But the mind could, as he came to believe, penetrate even to the temple of unreality in which the worshippers were so numerous. They were the people to be won. In the Socialist meeting-hall he met only the elect; in the theatre were the electors—fools, perhaps, but fools with votes.

The penetration was a slow process but it succeeded. Shaw made more converts to his various creeds as a playwright than ever he did as a pamphleteer. Encountering the work of Ibsen had been a powerful encouragement to making fact-finding and pamphleteering for the Fabians, which he dutifully continued, of less importance in his

The British Museum, early readers

life than the invasion of the theatre, that stronghold of the lies about life and the bourgeois self-deception which Ibsen had exposed and which he would further destroy by ridicule. But before he could create a new drama he had to earn a living by sitting in judgment on the old.

Shaw's introduction to writing about the London theatre was curiously untheatrical. It came through his early addiction to the works of Karl Marx. In the reading-room of the British Museum, which was one of the Poor Men's Colleges in Shaw's self-made University, he used to plough through the heavy soil of Marx's *Das Kapital,* using a French translation since he was not then and never became expert in German. It may not have been burdensome to a keen young Socialist who was much impressed at first but came later on to reject Marxian economics. He was to be seen studying as an alternative, and possibly as a relief, the scores of Wagnerian opera. In 1885 he was thus discovered by another serious reader, William Archer, a Scot with Norwegian family connections who had been fascinated by the plays of Ibsen. An acquaintance ensued which became a life-long friendship and an Ibsenite alliance. Here were uncommon brains and a common cause.

Shaw was then, at the age of twenty-nine and after nine years as a free-lance novelist and journalist, continuing to face complete professional failure and to endure poverty with nonchalance. London, he said, 'refused to tolerate me on any terms'. Archer took him in hand and got him some book reviewing for the *Pall Mall Gazette*. In the course of that work he discussed in January, 1886, a book on Shakespeare's Sonnets written by Thomas Tyler, another Museum reader. Tyler was a strange character, fantastically ugly and afflicted with a monstrous goitre. He held a hideous conception of the universe which he called the theatre of the cycles according to which history repeated itself immutably and for ever with human lives recurring in identical forms. If that were true, as Shaw observed, poor Tyler must have been suffering from that goitre through the ages and would continue to endure it through still more ages to come.

When not theorizing about the recurrent doom of mankind Tyler argued, and to his own satisfaction proved, that the 'lovely boy', the male recipient of the Sonnets, was the Earl of Pembroke and the Dark Lady Mary Fitton, the Queen's Maid of Honour who was disgraced by an affair with the wanton young Earl. Shaw described his congenial contact with Tyler in the Preface to *The Dark Lady of the Sonnets* in which brief play he presented Miss Fitton as the Lady. The dispute about the Sonnets and their background has gone rumbling on ever since and Miss Fitton is now somewhat out of favour; but she appealed strongly to Frank Harris and still has her supporters as well as the Shavian approval of his light-hearted trifle.

The two men got on well enough, talking about Shakespeare among other matters. Here, with Archer to discuss Ibsen and the theatre in general, was agreeable company; Archer was no Marxian but, like Shaw, he was radical in his general opinions and a keen anti-clerical. Tyler, like Shaw, was excited by Shakespeare. Outside the silence and solemnity of the reading-room the argument could flow. There was also the beginning of comparative prosperity, since Archer helped Shaw to earn one hundred and seventeen pounds in a year, an unprecedented achievement which would then buy him as much as seven or eight hundred pounds would do eighty years later.

For a review called *The World* Archer was both art critic and dramatic critic; he was self-conscious about the former post because he felt himself unqualified to be a judge of painting; drama was his subject. He persuaded the editor, Edmund Yates, to let Shaw take on the art criticism. On that subject he had some claim to write since the National Picture Gallery in Dublin had been one of the earliest of his centres of free education. He did not hesitate to accept the assignment which helped him to obtain other work.

By 1888 he had made himself sufficiently known as a clever new-comer in journalism to be taken on the staff of the evening paper, *The Star,* as a political writer. His chief, H. W. Massingham, later a brilliant editor of daily and weekly papers, was not one to inhibit the members of his staff or underrate originality. They need not toe the line, but they had to be somewhere near it and Shaw, in politics, was far out of Massingham's radical line and away to the Left. Instead of being dismissed as a nuisance he was turned on to music and his column signed Corno di Bassetto soon attracted attention. In 1890 he returned to *The World* and for the next four years wrote on music there under the well-known initials G.B.S.

When Yates died in 1894, Shaw suspected that no successor would be equally tolerant of his unorthodox views and methods. He resigned, but that involved no misfortune or hardship since Frank Harris engaged him as dramatic critic for *The Saturday Review* at a salary of six pounds a week. Even more important, he had ample space and freedom to go into unimpeded action, not only as a reviewer of individual productions but as an analyst and often an assailant of the persons and policies then dominant in theatrical affairs. Shaw, in gratitude, remained loyal to Harris amid all the latter's ups and downs of an astonishing and sometimes scandalous career. The editor had given his critic a small but discerning public and that authority was confirmed by the devastating brilliance of Shaw's articles on the drama of the day.

His first piece was written on December 29th, 1894, and his last on May 21st, 1898, when his health had broken down. His final sentences were, 'The younger generation is knocking at the door; and, as I open it, there steps spritely in the incomparable Max. For the rest, let Max speak for himself. I am off duty for ever and am going to sleep.' It was fortunately not wholly true. Max Beerbohm lived up to his welcome, but Shaw, far from remaining comatose, was to write theatrical criticism of a general and no less powerful kind in the Prefaces to his plays and other places. These, with some very early pieces, have been well assembled in a book called *Shaw On Theatre,* edited by Mr E. J. West.

Shaw's qualifications for writing about the theatre could then be called those of a failed playwright. He could also have claimed to review fiction with the same credentials. Between 1879 and 1883 he had been a novelist to the extent of five books which nobody would publish. Of his earliest experiment in drama he has recorded that it was a 'Passion Play with the mother of the hero represented as a termagant. I never carried it through'. Had he done so, it is unlikely that anybody would have carried it further.

He did not come into a critic's chair with the innocence and ignorance of stage matters which have been no bar to the entry of some recruits to the calling. As a boy he had been a regular playgoer in Dublin. During his youth in London he had seen and usually despised what he chose to see and could find the money to see. Moreover, he was already a practising playwright and, though rejected as most young dramatists are for a while, he had a high self-confidence and believed himself to be a natural dramatist with as much sense of theatre as zeal for Socialism.

Before Harris brought him to *The Saturday Review* he had written four plays which he later considered good enough (and which with one arguable exception were good enough) to be included as per-manencies in his complete published works. As the components of

27

his *Plays Unpleasant* they provide the first unit of a large and enduring series, the green-backed volumes known to myriads of readers. Only two of these pieces reached a public stage at that time. The first was *Widowers' Houses,* begun as an experiment in collaboration with William Archer. It was to be, thought Archer, an ordinary piece for a conventional and possibly commercial production. But Shaw had no idea of keeping to any 'please-the-public' rules and of meeting the needs of the market. He bewildered his colleague by turning an intended entertainment into a trenchant exposure.

The subject was landlordism and rack-renting. True to his principle that drama must be didactic Shaw injected into his love story of a young doctor and a rich man's daughter a powerful indictment of respectable people who lived on the payments wrung from very poor people for tenancies of housing worse than poor. The owners were shown doing so either as exploiters who knew what they were doing and did it without shame or as remote possessors of family property who were completely and inexcusably ignorant about the ugly source of their income. In discussing this topic Shaw was not merely a theorist; he had been a rent-collector in his Dublin boyhood. To attack such landlordism was good left-wing politics, but it was certainly not what theatre managers wanted. It appalled Archer who curiously failed to see any merit in the fresh outlook and pungency of Shaw's writing. An exposure of social iniquity masked by hypocrisy was surely exactly what that good Ibsenite and radical should have welcomed. But Archer's generally keen eye was strangely blind to the promise of a new and talented devotee of Ibsen's aims and methods.

Fortunately for Shaw a young, persistent enthusiast for unusual kinds of dramatic writing, J. T. Grein, arranged for a production by his Independent Theatre. The first night of *Widowers' Houses* at the Royalty Theatre was eventful. There were cheers and boos and a three-minute speech by the dramatist. There are some gruesome minutes, once customary but now rare on the English stage, when the author, who has spent some panic-stricken hours during the

Frank Harris   *J. T. Grein*

opening performance watching the impassive reception of his supposedly strong situations or brilliant thrusts of wit, appears after the
final curtain to mumble his gratitude to audience and artists and
possibly to receive the humiliation of a hiss. The after-curtain speech
was turned by Shaw's readiness with the right word into an entertainment instead of an embarrassment. The play failed to last but its
subject started a brisk discussion in the Press and put Shaw in the
news, a position which he was to sustain throughout his life, more
often to his enjoyment than not. Harris was not enlisting the
unknown nobody which Shaw had been a few years earlier.

Two of the other early plays had remained unacted in a public
theatre when the author turned critic. *The Philanderer,* concerned
with the amours and clashes of the 'advanced' types, male and
female, whom Shaw had met, has never been popular. It is the
weakest piece in the canon. When Shaw re-read it in later life he
dismissed it as 'a mixture of mechanical farce with realistic filth'.
Farcical perhaps, but filthy it is not. But then the permissible themes

and forms of speech were narrowly confined. The third play *Mrs Warren's Profession* was banned by the Censor because its central figure was an ex-prostitute who had become a prosperous brothel-keeper with a wealthy clientèle.

The patrons of the fashionable London theatres were well aware of the Mrs Warrens and their professional activities. Victorian society, though prim on the surface, had its core of sexual indulgence and promiscuity and this was common knowledge in more areas than Mayfair. But what was gossiped about and even gloated over was not to be exposed on the stage. The Censor was there to prevent such unmannerly candour and veracity and his discipline was not resented by the public which expected sex in plays to be either a demonstration of menaced but triumphant purity in melodrama or a bubble of champagne in comedy. If the Censor stopped the vinegary comments of a Socialist Puritan he was regarded as earning his keep by silencing one of the tiresome trouble-makers.

The fourth play of this period, *Arms and the Man,* was produced with capital provided by Miss A. E. F. Horniman, the remarkable pioneer and benefactress. After her support of the Abbey Theatre in Dublin she made stage history again by her backing of repertory seasons at the Gaiety Theatre in Manchester where social realism was the aim and the discovery of new dramatists a result. It lacked wide popular support. It never lacked ideas and intelligence. Grein had made possible a few performances of *Widowers' Houses* for the club members subscribing to his Independent Theatre. By renting the Royalty Theatre in London and staging the uncensored comedy which was Shaw's latest work, Miss Horniman introduced him to the general public at considerable cost to herself. She drew her private income, which was not immense, from her family's sales-manship of tea, thus giving to the art of Dionysus the profits derived from 'the cup that cheers but not inebriates'. *Arms and the Man* ran for a while at a loss. It was, however, liked when Richard Mansfield made it part of his repertory in the United States and has been one of the most popular of Shaw's pieces ever since. It was the first of the comedies published in the second volume of the Shavian canon, *Plays Pleasant*.

In the eighteen-nineties and for some time after book production was extremely cheap—'paperbacks' could be issued for a penny. For the juvenile readers there was a series called *Books for the Bairns* issued at that price and there were *Penny Classics* too. Since printing and paper were so cheap the probability of a small sale did not deter a publisher from producing collected theatrical revues by a leading critic and, despite the narrowness of the market, he could do so without loss, a practice now found to be impossible. The firm of Walter Scott, which handled Archer's translations of Ibsen, did this valuable service for his notices of plays.

To the 1894 volume Shaw wrote an introduction in which he described the theatrical conditions of the time. His purpose was to explain the problems of management to the intellectuals who 'though interested in the art of the theatre neither know nor care anything about the business of the theatre'. He was no detached theorist scolding the managers for not putting on propagandist plays wanted only by the friends of the author and the few devotees of theatrical progress or a political cause. He knew that the art of the theatre has to live as best it can in a corner of the large industry of entertainment.

For its residents and visitors in 1895 central London had about two dozen playhouses usually occupied. Now there are about forty serving a much greater surrounding population and a much greater influx of visitors. But the suburbs had, or were acquiring, a ring of their own theatres, capacious and comfortable houses with very cheap prices for their seats; in them the playgoer could go to the stalls or balcony for three shillings or so. To them came touring companies including some of the most popular. Often on view were Fred Terry and Julia Neilson with their romantic costume plays, the kind of thing that Shaw detested and the public did not. As a boy, and not Shavian and Ibsenite, I could do myself very well for very little money at one of these houses, the Camden Theatre at Mornington Crescent.

The Old Vic had nothing to attract the attention of Shaw the critic at that time. Founded as the Coburg Theatre in 1818, it had first offered spectacular drama with occasional Shakespeare, including some appearances of Edmund Kean. Later it was a music-hall and a somewhat rough and rowdy house, frequented by hard drinkers. Rescued for popular culture and sobriety by Miss Emma Cons, the aunt of her famous successor Lilian Baylis, its purpose was to be 'a cheap and decent place of amusement on strict temperance lines'. Good music and lectures among the coffee and buns were the fare provided. Opera at popular prices came to the Waterloo Road in 1900, Shakespeare not until 1914. The Shakespearian presentations which Shaw had to write about were either lavishly produced for runs in a West End theatre or occasional productions by an ascetic and wholly uncommercial enthusiast, William Poel. These were given on bare platforms in halls and attended by quite small audiences of Poel's supporters. Shaw on Shakespeare and the contrasted Shakespearian methods of Irving and Poel will be discussed later.

The four-and-twenty West End playhouses were mainly tenanted by actor-managers. There was no need for the large capital investment which such ventures would need today. Shaw explained that a London actor playing leading parts in the eighteen-nineties drew for his salary between twenty to forty pounds a week and that out of this he could in a few years save enough to try the experiment of taking a theatre for a few months in which he could be his own master. He usually had to have a 'backer' to add to the meagre capital on which he could begin. The risk seems trifling compared with the huge gamble that theatrical investment has become.

The entire cost of renting a central theatre, staging a contemporary play, and paying the company (not, of course, in a mammoth Shakespearian treat for the public eye or a musical piece with a chorus) could be as low as four hundred pounds a week. This included two or three changes of scene, which the audience expected for its money, as well as a small orchestra, then deemed an essential amenity, rendering its light music before the curtain rose and during the intervals.

Even if the takings needed to 'break even' were as high as six hundred pounds a week the outlay seems astonishingly small to us amid the inflationary finance of the nineteen-sixties when a short three-act piece with only a single set and quite a small cast will have to draw over three thousand pounds a week in order to avoid loss.

The price of stalls in the West End was then as high as half-a-guinea. (The very popular Squire Bancroft with his talented wife Marie Wilton had raised it to that level thirty years earlier and, while improving actors' salaries, he had made enough to retire at the age of forty-five.) Thus an actor-manager who was careful and could carry on and make both ends meet with receipts of four hundred pounds a week had only to sell eight hundred stalls during his eight performances. The rest of the house provided an agreeable surplus. Shaw calculated that by averaging the prices between a shilling for the gallery and ten and sixpence for the stalls, with a price list ranging through balcony, upper circle, and pit, the general level of payment for admission was about five shillings.

Thus even a lavish venture, whose running costs were six hundred pounds a week, was financially viable if two thousand four hundred people came to see it in the eight performances: a more economical undertaking could keep alive on proportionately less. To attract three hundred to each session should not seemingly have been diffi-cult, unless of course the author was new and the play unusual, as was the case with *Arms and the Man*. This was kept on for eleven weeks between the April and July of 1894 and in all took less than eighteen hundred pounds with an average of just over twenty-three pounds for each performance. Miss Horniman had put up four thousand pounds in all. Shaw calculated that if all its patrons had come in the first fortnight and the show had then closed, the backer would have done quite well. But that is not how theatre-life works. Playgoers are naturally dilatory and wait for a recommendation by word of mouth in doubtful cases. Only an occasional 'smash hit' is packed from the start. Often there has to be a period of nursing the infant production in the hope of a large and steady growth to follow.

33

Shaw's early plays proved to be very late developers in every case.

Shaw realized that without the actor-managers there would be hardly any theatre in central London at that time. The drama's patrons give the drama's laws and these patrons were voting for personalities and not for plays, a habit of long endurance; we still need the 'box-office names'. Then few were interested by Shakespeare without lavish trimmings and magnetic personalities, but many were more than interested and were spellbound by Shakespearian productions with Irving and Ellen Terry. There had to be the big name in the big part and a big show of scenery as well. Shaw pointed out that if Irving were to produce a tragedy or Wyndham a comedy in which they took subordinate parts, however well suited to them, the public would stay away 'and the author of the piece would have reason to curse the self-denial of the actor-manager'. Shaw's theatrical idealism did not prevent him from being a realist about its rewards.

So the star system was inevitable. There were no state subsidies for a national or municipal theatre and none to come for another fifty years. The normal payer of rates and taxes and the Councillors and Members of Parliament whom he elected would tolerate public support of libraries, museums, and art galleries, but the playhouse was thought to be just what its frivolous name implied, a box of tricks and toys, some of them demoralizing. Let the players behave themselves and feed themselves. Why should these triflers be given doles? The traditional belief of the Puritans about the wickedness of theatrical illusion and the folly of 'let's pretend' was still powerful. Play-acting was in the eyes of many solid citizens the devil's trade; at its most respectable, as at Irving's Lyceum, it could attract an illustrious audience, including prominent statesmen, to its first nights. There could be nothing shameful where Mr Gladstone took his seat. But none of the politicians would have dared to vote a penny of public funds to help Irving cope with the burden of his costs and face the risk of an expensive production which failed to please; and of these he had his share. He died a poor man.

It cost nothing to reward him with the theatre's first knighthood. This occurred in the initial year of Shaw's work in criticism. While saying that he cared nothing for public titles and honours, which he himself always refused, Shaw welcomed the tribute to Sir Henry as a belated admission of the drama's dignity and importance. Fifty years later the nation obtained its Arts Council whose funds for the sustenance and development of the arts were at first small but grew rapidly. By the middle of the century town councils were beginning to spend public money, a procedure legalized by the Labour Government in 1948, on theatres as well as on museums. The Dickensian Alderman Cute had a passion for Putting Down anything deemed unnecessary by himself and he would have put down any play-acting as provoking idleness among the workers. But now the Cutes had so far changed their minds as to start Putting Up.

Harley Granville-Barker   *William Archer*

The idea of a National Theatre, a familiar institution in most European capitals, had been urged as a necessity for Britain by Charles Dickens and a few others fifty years earlier. Shaw was naturally one of its champions, but here the Cutes were tenacious in their antagonism. Nothing was done till 1962 and then two committees were formed to plan its establishment with public money. Since agreement as to the architecture of the new building was slow, a National Theatre Company, amply endowed, took over the Old Vic under the direction of Sir Laurence Olivier in 1963 as a temporary home. Thus the cause for which Shaw, Archer, and Granville-Barker had worked strenuously was to win a tardy victory after the death of all three.

Back in the eighteen-nineties the actor-managers were keeping the country as well as London supplied with plays according to popular demand. Indeed, the provincial cities were far better off than they are now. The leading players went on tour regularly, taking out their pieces which had pleased the capital instead of travelling for a few weeks with untried ones for which they now use the provincials as tasters. In large towns there were two or more theatres of size receiving a wide variety of companies; now there is probably only one of these surviving in each and in many places of considerable size there is not even that. Fortunately the construction and endowment of civic theatres is spreading and the place of the distinguished visitor is being taken by younger resident teams presenting a repertory often of a quite adventurous and novel kind. If Shaw had been a young dramatic critic today he would have found himself continually on the move to consider new productions in the more important provincial 'reps'. He made few journeys out of London for *The Saturday Review* because there was only rarely the need to see what was happening outside the capital. In the great majority of his professional attendances he was confronting the cluster of London's actor-managers.

Thus the kind of drama which he had to review was strictly limited by theatrical finance and the dictation of public taste. The actor-manager had to have a long part rich in opportunities and of the type which he could best exploit. That, Shaw frankly admitted, was inevitable if the audiences put magnetic personality first and serious portrayal of life a bad second. Inevitably the star system tied the authors' hands. They had so to shape their work in order to include a 'hero' part suitably sympathetic; if the leading role were unheroic or even villainous, it had to be that of a picturesque scoundrel with abundant scope for the more lurid kind of character. In comedies it was essential that smart life with fashionable dresses for the ladies should be portrayed. For that kind of theatre Shaw admitted the financial excuse, but to it he would certainly not contribute.

He could not have been more frank on that point. In the Preface to his second volume, *Plays Pleasant,* he wrote, 'I have no grievance against our theatres' and added that he had heaped difficulties in the way of achieving performance of his work by deliberately ignoring the managers and their customers. But he could no more write what they wanted than 'Joachim could put aside his fiddle and oblige a happy company of bean-feasters with a marching tune on the German concertina. They must keep away from my plays; that is all'. For a long time they obeyed that instruction; they kept away.

CHAPTER THREE

Shaw and Shakespeare

THE supporters of the National Theatre had thought of it as a Shakespeare Memorial. Despairing with sufficient reason of a state grant for building and a subsidy for maintenance, they appealed to a public whose ear remained deaf to the supplications. One rich man made a handsome donation; the less rich could only help by subscribing small sums in large numbers and this they failed to do. As G. K. Chesterton summed up the situation in a laughing rhyme:

> And while the vain world careless sped
> Unheeding the heroic name—
> The souls most fed with Shakespeare's flame
> Still sat unconquered in a ring
> Remembering him like anything.

Among these rememberers and active in the cause were Shaw, William Archer, and that brilliant actor and director of plays, Granville-Barker. In 1910 Shaw contributed to 'a performance in aid of the funds of the project for establishing a National Theatre as a memorial to Shakespear' (he preferred that spelling). For the occasion he wrote his very entertaining one-act piece *The Dark Lady of the Sonnets* whom he identified, remembering Mr Tyler as well as Shakespeare, as Mistress Fitton.

If Shaw had despised Shakespeare as a dramatist and had detested all tributes to the Bard, as he certainly detested the empty verbal adulation which he called Bardolatry, he would hardly have troubled to serve this cause. The idea of Shaw as a Shakespeare-hater, although quite misleading, did not spring up without some cause. In his dramatic criticism for *The Saturday Review* he had written in terms of devastating contempt for Shakespeare's intellectual capacities. In his criticism of Sir Henry Irving's production of *Cymbeline* in September, 1896, he had been so galled both by the play and its production that he lashed out at Shakespeare's 'pretentious reduction of life's subtlest problems to common-places against which a Polytechnic debating club would revolt' and at the 'sententious combination of ready reflection with complete intellectual sterility'. 'With the single exception of Homer,' Shaw continued, 'there is no eminent writer, not even Sir Walter Scott, whom I can despise so entirely as I despise Shakespear.'

There was more in the same vein which has been much quoted. Less often, and perhaps never quoted, is the beginning of the next paragraph: 'But I am bound to add that I pity the man who cannot enjoy Shakespear. He has outlasted thousands of abler thinkers and will outlast thousands more.' He went on to praise the enormous power shown in his use of language, his humour, his gigantic stores of energy, and his capacity to make imaginary scenes and people more real to us than actual life. Shaw's knowledge of Shakespeare, almost line by line, was prodigious, and he could assert that when he was twenty he knew the Shakespearian characters, from Hamlet down even to a small part like that of the executioner Abhorson, more intimately than he knew his own living contemporaries.

Why then his explosion of fury released by Irving's *Cymbeline*? At the age of ninety-three, and near to his death, he did me the great honour and kindness of writing to me, with additions in his own hand, a long letter about Shakespeare. This was the result of his reading a book of mine published in that year. He began by a compliment which, coming from him, could have turned the head of any biographer, and went on to say: 'You are just as bardolatrous as myself, except that I began with *Cassells' Illustrated Family Shakespeare* at the age of ten and never had an academic set-back.' This was a reference to my own and the fairly general experience of school-time exasperation with Shakespeare caused by dreary teaching and the turning of his plays into curriculum items and holiday tasks.

I had, unfairly as I think now, quoted some of the denunciation in the *Cymbeline* review. He ended his letter which advised some alterations and deletions with these words:

'If my hackneyed outburst about *Cymbeline* must be dragged in, it should not be dismissed as an anti-Stratford blasphemy. It raises the problem of how it came to be written, not by Greene, or Dr Johnson, or Byron, or Morris, who were none of them bardolators, but by me, who, like yourself, was and is among the most bardolatrous of all the bardolators. The solution is that the fury and scurrility of the

Henry Irving

anti-Ibsen persecution and the praise by the press critics of Irving's and Daly's mutilations of Shakespear's plays made it so evident that they had never read a line of them that it was necessary to debunk Shakespear as well as extol Ibsen. Your book needs a new chapter dealing with the blow dealt to Shakespearism by the advent of Ibsen and Strindberg, which could not be ignored as the advent of Goethe had been.

'I dare not write any more. I think I have said all that can be of any use to you. Read at your leisure if you ever have any; and forgive'

The scurrilous vituperation of Ibsen had been at its height when J. T. Grein arranged for a production of *Ghosts* in March, 1891. The play did not get, and in those times could not expect to get, a licence for public performance. It exposed the private life of a public man, the debauched Alving who passed as 'a good fellow' and respectable citizen thanks to his wife's concealment of his conduct and her sufferings. The play contained a seduced maidservant, an illegitimate daughter, the possibility of incest, and a case of venereal disease. This was inherited by Alving's son Oswald who ends the story as a doomed young man in the first stages of general paralysis of the insane.

The Lord Chamberlain, acting as Censor of Plays (there has never been a separate person called the Censor in the British Establishment) must have known that such people and such calamities exist. He could not fail to know that, according to the Second Commandment of the religion of his country, 'the Lord thy God is a jealous God and visits the sins of the fathers on the children unto the third and fourth generation'. Ibsen was but confirming the law and the prophets. But in late Victorian England, and indeed in England for some time after, it was the rule that such things, though known, should not be seen to be known and openly mentioned. Least of all should such exposures be made in the theatre where sex was then acceptable only as a theme for romantic flapdoodle, melodramatic fustian, or salacious comedy of a frenchified kind which invited guffaws at the neat contrivance of adulterous intrigue or sniggers at the dialogue full of *doubles entendres*.

This was the drama of the day which Shaw despised and hated and which the voluptuaries in the audience, who may have included a few Alvings among them, relished and crowded to see. The Lord Chamberlain let the sniggerers have what they wanted. What the realists and Ibsenites wanted, in their eagerness to use the theatre for exposing the shams as well as the sins of society, could only be seen at private performances. These were free of censorship if no money was taken at the doors and the audience came in as subscribing members of a playgoers' club or as recipients of free seats. Here was a loophole through which the progressives could escape from the general ban. Through it Grein could proceed to evade the Censor and show to his associates and supporters a play well known in Europe and available in print in England to any who chose to read it.

He invited the critics to see his production of *Ghosts*. To call their response to the receipt of 'complimentary tickets' complimentary is as far from the truth as may be. Most of them did not criticize Ibsen's way of lifting the roof from Alving's apparently happy and respectable household. They raved and cursed. The reviews in some papers seemed not so much to be printed as carried foaming into the street. William Archer collected these absurdities in an article called *Ghosts and Gibberings* and Shaw quoted abundant specimens of these gibberings in his book on *The Quintessence of Ibsenism*. The play was called 'an open drain, a loathesome sore unbandaged, a lazar-house with all its doors and windows open'. It was 'gross, fetid, putrid'. Even the *Radical Press,* in which some tolerance of innovation might have been expected, wrote of 'wicked loathesomeness' and 'a repulsive and degrading work'. There were further charges of 'noisome corruption' and demands for legal prosecution. The native Ibsenites, as much as Ibsen, came in for a similar drenching in reckless abuse. They were called 'prurient cranks'. They were denounced as 'unsexed females' and 'much-ferreting dogs'. It was twenty-three years later that people were permitted to see *Ghosts* at a licensed performance in a public theatre. At last the 'open drain' was accepted as a channel of salutary warning and instruction.

Shaw was naturally nauseated by the stupidity of those who could not realize that this was a grimly moral play and as powerful a warning against dissipated lives and sexual indulgence as could possibly be uttered. He was infuriated too by the cant of the critics who praised the comedy of sniggers and raged at the people who wanted to bring the English theatre up to date. The Free Theatre movement, a revolt against the stale and puerile entertainments of the commercial theatre, was advancing in the foreign capitals. It appealed to a minority, but the minority soon grew in numbers and was not subject to censorship or vexed with persecution. Shaw and others such as Grein and Archer were attempting to end an insularity which they thought to be ridiculous and a discipline which degraded and put fetters upon theatrical authorship and theatrical production, thus keeping the country far behind the times and ludicrous in the eyes of the world.

The vituperations hurled at Ibsen in England were accompanied by the conventional veneration of Shakespeare. Shaw, as he explained, decided that 'it was necessary to de-bunk Shakespear as well as extol Ibsen'. There is some lack of logic here. It seems unfair to Shakespeare that he should be ridiculed and damned for the intemperate bardolatry which he never sought or expected. (A man who does not bother to preserve the text of half of his own plays is not courting the plaudits and the worship of posterity.) But one can read between the words the grievance that was rankling in Shaw's mind. Ibsen was an acute and consistent thinker; Shakespeare was a spasmodic thinker, finding, it is true, the perfect word for the casual thought or feeling. He was a brilliant analyst of human nature but he was not examining the structure of society with the penetration of a left-wing social reformer.

Accordingly for Shaw, himself at the time a Socialist rebel, speaker, and writer, Ibsen not Shakespeare was the man who mattered. Bardolatry was the pestilence that must be crushed and in the crushing process deemed necessary Shakespeare's mental capacities were scoffed at because they were rated far below Ibsen's.

Damning a writer for failing in a field where he never attempted to succeed is a common fault of criticism and Shaw in his well-justified rage at the idiotic reception of Ibsen in England fell into that error. Shakespeare, as a member of the Lord Chamberlain's, later the King's, Men for more than twenty years and as such a Groom of the Royal Chamber, was part of the Establishment and therefore considered himself to be an entertainer, not a lecturer on politics and economics. In the epilogue to *The Tempest,* generally taken to be a kind of farewell message to the public, Prospero expressly says 'since my project was to please'—not, be it noted, to preach. That line is too often overlooked by those who visualize Shakespeare as a man with a load of moral messages.

It was also unreasonable to harp on Shakespeare's omission to anticipate Ibsen as an iconoclast destroying the hypocritical idealism of the bourgeois. What had driven Shaw into the fit of temper which animated his attack on Irving's *Cymbeline* were the managerial methods more than the quality of the Bard's brain-power. He objected to the cutting and re-shaping, and sometimes wanton titivation, of the plays practised at that time. There was nothing new in such malpractice. As soon as the theatre was restored to life by the restoration of the monarchy in 1660 Shakespeare's work was regarded as adaptable and was drastically adapted with no sense of shame.

When Samuel Pepys saw *Macbeth* in 1667 he judged it to be 'one of the best plays for a stage and variety of dancing and musick that ever I saw'. Dryden with D'Avenant, who claimed to be Shakespeare's illegitimate son, re-wrote *The Tempest* introducing new characters, including Dorinda, who is Miranda's sister. A little later Nahum Tate, a hymn-writer and versifier of the Psalms, took *King Lear* in hand and made the mightiest of tragedies end happily with 'a success for the innocent distressed persons'. It was also a success for actors and audiences. This version held the stage until the middle of the nineteenth century and was defended even by Dr Johnson who found the death of Cordelia an unbearable shock. The comedies were frequently turned into musicals as they still sometimes are. That Shakespeare might have enjoyed *Kiss Me Kate,* a recent romp made out of *The Taming of the Shrew,* is possible. That he would have approved of Nahum Tate is beyond belief; yet Garrick, who revered Shakespeare and organized the first Shakespeare Festival at Stratford-upon-Avon, played the 'happy ending' version of *Romeo and Juliet* as well as of *King Lear.*

These alterations, first made, as Dryden said, to suit 'a more refined age' to whom Shakespeare seemed rough and barbarous, were continued and increased during the two centuries following the Restoration. In his long mid-Victorian years at Sadler's Wells, Edmund Phelps made a return to the original texts. What manipulations and, according to Shaw, mutilations of the plays were made by Irving were trifles compared with what had gone on before; the titivations made by Augustin Daly, ridiculed by Shaw, were added only to some comedies of which Shaw had a poor opinion. So his grievance was nothing like that of an eighteenth-century Shakespearian devotee eager for the play as it had been written, and then faced with the botched versions which, with the persuasive power of Garrick's acting applied to them, made the all-conquering David secure in his supremacy on the English stage.

Augustin Daly was a man of Irish-American stock who began life as a journalist in New York and became a dramatic critic at the age of twenty-one, thus learning about the theatre while precociously sitting in judgment on his seniors. In 1869, when he was thirty, he felt that he knew enough about the subject to give up precept for practice. He found backers, went into management, and remained a popular and flourishing impresario and a minor dramatist until his death in 1899. In the latter part of his career he was responsible for many productions in London where he also organized the building of a playhouse carrying his own name, as he had done in New York. Daly's Theatre in Leicester Square, on the site where the Warner Theatre now stands, was to become famous for its musical comedies. On its stage the hearts of fair ladies broke in waltz-time and were no less melodiously mended before the night was out. That was after Shaw's critical years and romance of the blue Danubian kind was not for him. But the tradition of the house was being maintained since, as he put it, Daly had made vaudeville of Shakespeare in the eighteen-nineties.

The gardens of the Square were made public property by the generosity of a company promoter, Albert Grant, M.P., in 1874, two years before Shaw came to London. When he arrived the centre of the Square had become a depository for dead cats and junk of all kinds. Mr Grant put an end to a public disgrace in a town then tolerant of filth. The benefactor also embellished his gift with a marble fountain and a copy of the statue of Shakespeare by Peter Scheemakers which stands in the Poets' Corner of Westminster Abbey. Thus the Bard, presented as a pensive figure facing Daly's Theatre, could be seen as it were surveying the façade if not the

operations within. Since Shakespeare in stone is now entirely surrounded by cinemas where once were theatres, a logical case could
be made for removing his image to a more suitable spot, possibly the
South Bank of the Thames, and substituting one of Mr Goldwyn or
the Warner Brothers.

Yet, while Shaw railed at Daly for his 'vaudeville' versions of
Shakespeare, he could thank him for one thing at least: he introduced Ada Rehan to British audiences. She too was American-Irish
and she had power to enchant. Of her performance as Rosalind in
As You Like It he wrote: 'her voice, compared to Sarah Bernhardt's
voix d'or, has been as all the sounds of woodland to the clinking of
twenty-franc pieces. In Shakespear (or what Mr Daly leaves of him)
she was and is irresistible'. Those were strong words from one then
more noted for his damning than his blessing of the players. For the
rearranged text and the music which accompanied the principal
speeches of Adam, Jacques, and Rosalind as well as the songs, Shaw
condemned Daly to permanent exile. He charitably suggested
St Helena.

The absurdities of Augustin included the transposition of songs
from one of Shakespeare's plays to another. In *Twelfth Night* which
Shaw saw when he was a music critic in 1894, a chorus, made up,
it seemed to G.B.S., of Illyria's lodging-house keepers, appeared
promptly on the sea-coast to sing Ariel's 'Come unto these yellow
sands'. 'Who is Sylvia?' was later introduced with an alteration to
'Who is Olivia?'. The exquisite 'Come away, death' was dropped
altogether—too sad, presumably, for a comedy. Shakespeare had to
be taught his trade. *The Two Gentlemen of Verona* is an early and
ineffective comedy never much liked, even in its youth. (We hear of
no performance or printing of it in Quarto during Shakespeare's
lifetime.) Today, even with all our observance of textual fidelity, we
should not be horrified by some directors' tricks designed to cover
its weakness. Shaw protested at the ridiculous notions of Italian
architecture in the décor, but Ada Rehan was there and wore down
his indignation since he kindly admitted that, after all, the Daly

hotchpotch provided 'a very pleasant entertainment for those who know no better'.

In Daly's version of *A Midsummer Night's Dream* the parts of Oberon and Puck were both played by women. Duke Theseus was shown in a 'panoramic' progress to Athens on a barge. The age of electricity had arrived and so the fairies carried torches with portable batteries and switched them off and on, 'like children with a new toy'. The feminine but fairly agile Puck had a trapeze for a gymnastic display. The text, of course, was chopped about to display Daly's manner of handling a carving knife.

Shaw's quarrel with Sir Henry Irving was of a more complicated kind. Here he was in conflict with a great man, a great actor, and a great influence. Daly was seen and ridiculed in a quite good-tempered way as a commercial manager who thought he could be cultural and popular at the same time by putting plenty of sugar on the Shakespearian pill. Irving, although he had to work without subsidy in the commercial theatre, was never a man on the make. Shaw could not complain that he cared too much about money; he did complain that the leader of the British stage cared too much about himself. The charge was that Irving treated the Bard as a background to his own performances, overloading the stage and slowing down the action with a multitude of scene changes and rearranging episodes in the plays to please himself. Part of Shaw's grievance was that Irving was a mangler who dismembered the play and the poetry. But there was further cause for his indignation.

Shaw, as a zealous Ibsenite and champion of the New Drama, wanted Irving to participate in the changes which were gathering pace in the European capitals and lagging and indeed scarcely stirring in London. It would be a triumph if Irving would see the light that had been kindled in Oslo. Surely, he thought, the leader should be leading and leading to the Left. Also vexatious to Shaw was the waste, as he thought, of the shining talents and personality of Ellen Terry.

Even more than Ada Rehan, Ellen Terry had enchanted him. But

Ellen Terry

he deemed the parts which she played in her long association with Irving at the Lyceum Theatre unworthy of this wonderful woman and mistress of her craft. While as a critic Shaw kept strictly to his side of the curtain and did not meet his ideal actress, he began a lengthy and brilliant correspondence in which she could hold her own. He sent her his ideas about the roles which she took or was to take. Furthermore he did not limit himself to advising Ellen Terry and censuring Irving; he wrote his one-act play about Napoleon and a Strange Lady called *The Man of Destiny* specially for them. Irving considered it at leisure and then offered Shaw fifty pounds for an option on it. This Shaw refused on principle because he regarded managerial payments for options on plays by journalists as a form of bribery, which indeed in certain cases they were. Victorian dramatic critics were used to this device; they knew that their pieces were unlikely ever to be produced, but some were ready to take money and with it the hint as to their future appraisals.

In the end Irving never staged *The Man of Destiny*. Shaw wrote *Captain Brassbound's Conversion* with Ellen Terry in mind for the rich part of Lady Cecily. She never played it. Irving seemed to be always in the way, leaving Ibsen to the obscure and solitary productions by the faithful, squandering the radiant capacities of Ellen Terry, and continuing to present Shakespeare exactly as Shaw did not like it and the public usually did.

The idea that Shaw never spoke well of Irving is nonsense. When he took over his assignment at *The Saturday Review* the third article that he wrote was on the production of *King Arthur* by J. Comyns

Carr at the Lyceum Theatre in January, 1895, in one scene of which, as he wrote, 'Mr Irving rises to the height of his art and impersonates with the noblest feeling and most sensitive refinement of execution the King Arthur of all our imaginations.' The dramatist's attempts at poetry received a thrashing of true Shavian vigour, but Irving as an actor had nothing to grumble at. In Shakespeare's plays too Shaw said that he surpassed the old tradition and 'left Barry Sullivan and Macready half a century behind'. The cause of dispute was what Shaw considered falsifications of the plays, and this so enraged him as to make him increasingly hostile to the Irving régime and the authority conferred on all that he did by the veneration of the public. Hence came the scathing review of Irving's *Cymbeline* including the remarks about Shakespeare's mind which became notorious. That Shaw should subsequently explain that he had to debunk Shakespeare because the critics and the public would take anything from Daly and Irving only shows that in the eighteen-nineties he allowed his temper to put reason out of court.

Shaw was extremely contemptuous of Irving's acting in some non-Shakespearian work, especially as the old soldier, Corporal Brewster, in a short play by Conan Doyle called *The Story of Waterloo*. As in *The Bells* Irving was here unashamedly the actor acting; going into action, as it were with the flags flying and drums beating, he achieved an almost hypnotic power over the audience. But Shaw was proof against any spellbinding by an actor; to the captivating qualities of an actress he often succumbed. Sarah Bernhardt was the exception. Her flamboyance was as unlikable to him as Irving's. Laurence Irving in his admirable life of his grandfather summed up acutely the difference between the two men. Both were egoists. Both were passionately interested in their work and in the theatre. But the realism of the one and the romanticism of the other made them completely incompatible. Of Shaw Laurence Irving wrote:

'He liked actors well enough as long as they were content to follow the directions of a puppet-dangling playwright. Bravura acting left him unmoved; he was unable to comprehend what Irving described as the actor's power "to arouse the intelligence by the vibrations and modulations of organized sound". He was constitutionally immune to the spell which an actor of genius can, with the poorest literary material, cast upon his audience; his allergy to the world of romantic illusion upon which the curtain of the Lyceum rose was incurable. His insusceptibility to the forces which have sustained the art of acting through centuries, often barren of dramatic literature, was as inherent as Irving's inability to understand the new generation of playwrights who would use the stage as a platform for the dissemination of their social and political doctrines.'

From this clash of tastes and temperaments came the hammering of Shakespeare for want of consistent thinking and the angry denigration which Shaw was later on to regret, to explain, and to withdraw.

While Shakespeare's plays were being swaddled in scenery to the point, as Shaw thought, of suffocation, one man was stripping them and doing that so thoroughly that Mr Bridges-Adams in his excellent book *The Irresistible Theatre* spoke of him as a Nudist. That was William Poel whose methods Shaw blessed as heartily as he cursed those of Irving. Poel, who changed his name from Pole because his father objected to his becoming an actor, had a curious start to a career of artistic austerity and powerful, if belated, influence. For two years he was manager of the Old Vic Theatre which was to become a Shakespearian temple; but then it was a music-hall. He found work more suited to his taste and talents when he became instructor to a Shakespeare Reading Society of which Shaw wrote in May, 1895, 'I have seen these suburban amateurs seated like Christy minstrels on the platform of the lecture hall at the London Institution produce, at a moderate computation, about sixty-six times as much effect by reading through *Much Ado About Nothing* as Mr Irving with his expensively mounted and superlatively dull Lyceum version.'

In 1894 Poel had been able, with some small financial aid, to found the Elizabethan Stage Society which in a life of eleven years produced on a bare stage the medieval morality called *Everyman* and a wide

William Poel as Keegan in JOHN BULL'S OTHER ISLAND, *Kingsway, 1912*

range of Elizabethan and Jacobean plays. The members of the Society were mostly amateurs trained by Poel. Shaw could not always approve their acting when he saw them, but he vigorously applauded the principle of an uncluttered stage and a direct attack on the audience. He could not claim that Poel refrained from cutting the text, for Poel was a Puritan in more than his artistic methods. He would omit words and lines that shocked him. But there was no hewing of the text of the kind practised by Daly and Irving.

Poel took his players to platforms of all kinds in buildings of all architectural periods. His company gave *The Comedy of Errors* in the hall of Gray's Inn and *The Tempest* in the Mansion House of London's Lord Mayor, to whom Shaw passed a grateful vote of thanks for being released from the usual 'guzzling horrors and insufferable oratory' customary in the banqueting chamber. He insisted that Shakespeare could always paint his scenery so vividly with his mastery of words as to make the supposed realism of the canvas sets then in vogue ridiculous. The same, he said, was true of a storm at sea. Poel, for his production of *The Tempest,* had no ship at all; there was the singers' gallery instead of a pretended vessel expensively built, mechanically rocked, and completely unconvincing. Shaw praised Poel for the successful spur to imagination achieved by leaving out the winds, waters, and creaking timbers and letting the waves come crashing through in Shakespeare's lines. He quoted 'What care these roarers for the name of king?' and added 'You see the white horses and the billowing green mountains playing football with crown and purple'. Further, he always appreciated the music of the past provided by Poel's constant allies, the Dolmetsch family, with viol and lute, virginals and viola da gamba. This was a welcome change from Daly and the music chosen for his vaudevilles.

Shaw was not a thorough-going Nudist of the Poel kind. He said, for example, that he could not welcome a stripped stage for *Othello* but he repeated that the more he saw of the Elizabethan Stage Society's work the more convinced he was that working on an open stage amidst the audience brought the play 'closer home to its hearers than when it is presented as a picture framed by a proscenium'. Poel, when his Society foundered, plodded on and I have seen him use a large music-hall with the front stalls covered over by planks to make a fore-stage as near to that of Shakespeare's time as he could contrive. He rarely had the kind of actors who draw a big public. He remained a lonely and dedicated figure, 'known to his own'. But his reputation grew and his methods, at least in part, prevailed half a century after his pioneering had begun. He was a victor in the long campaign of which Shaw was an early champion. Now the projecting stage with no drop-curtain and the minimum of scenery and scenic change is nearly always deemed essential to the production of a Shakespeare play. For Shaw, too, it was the victory of a strongly supported cause.

Misquotation or partial quotation has presented Shaw as an anti-Shakespearian. In fact he could far better have been called the very active President of a Society for the Prevention of Cruelty to Shakespeare. He did indeed take a poor view of the borrowed plots and the range of reflection in some of Shakespeare's plays. But, when challenged on this point in 1905, he stated clearly that in manner and art nobody could write better than Shakespeare because, carelessness apart, 'he did the thing as well as it can be done within the limits of human faculty'. The bardolators could hardly ask for more than that, and bardolator he proclaimed himself to be.

CHAPTER FOUR

Learning and Teaching

How many years are covered by the term Early Victorian? If it is applicable up to the death of the Prince Consort in 1861 Shaw had five years of this epoch. He was born three months after the end of the Crimean War. The Queen had completed the rebuilding of Balmoral Castle in 1855 and the news that Sebastopol had fallen came with its opening and was celebrated with bonfires and Highland revel. She and her husband decided that here was their paradise and that London life was so burdensome and sometimes so distasteful that long vacations on Deeside were an essential relief.

Landseer, happy as the royal guest and the Queen's tutor at the easel, was sovereign in the world of painting. Dickens, aged forty-four when Shaw was born, had moved into his last and favourite home at Gad's Hill, near Rochester. *Little Dorrit,* a book for which Shaw had an immense admiration since in his view it contained more revolutionary material than the entire works of Karl Marx, was coming out in parts. Charlotte Brontë had died the year before. Tennyson had just published *Maud* and was working on *The Idylls of the King.* Thackeray, having triumphed with his lectures on *The Four Georges,* was completing *The Virginians.* Macaulay was in full and powerful swing as the historian of England after the revolution against the last of the Stuarts. Matthew Arnold began his ten years as Professor of Poetry at Oxford University in 1857. The Brownings were established and Mrs Browning's *Aurora Leigh* appeared in 1856. In that year George Meredith emerged with *The Shaving of Shagpat.* Swinburne went to Balliol College, Oxford, in 1857 and to his chagrin failed to win the Newdigate Prize for poetry. Within the early years of Shaw's boyhood he had risen to shock some, fascinate many, especially the young, and fight for his later conquest. If Early Victorianism was ending, it was ending with amplitude and high achievement in letters. There were no repercussions across the Irish Channel. Ireland was vocal in politics; not for half a century did it remember Swift and become once more England's rival and even teacher in the art of writing English.

The education which Shaw received and despised in Dublin has been briefly described. If he had been born in England he would probably have fared no better. A national system of schooling for all was not created until 1872. The children of the workers were still getting what they could where they could and for what little they could pay and often that meant no education at all. Dickens had ended, or at least diminished, the scandals of the Yorkshire schools where Squeers and other scoundrels of his kind boarded and starved the unwanted children of parents who could afford to have these wretched brats taken off their hands. But the Creakles were still wielding their canes and making their fraudulent pretensions to pedagogy. As a specimen of the education to be got in the industrial

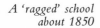

A 'ragged' school about 1850

towns Dickens in *Hard Times* (1854) had introduced to public attention the methods of Mr M'Choakumchild who, with the full
approval of Mr Gradgrind, was implanting facts, facts, facts, and
putting imagination high among the deadly sins.

Scarcely less dismal were the methods of Paul Dombey's genteel
academy at Brighton, where Dr and Miss Blimber killed any lively
stirrings of a young mind with languages 'dead, stone dead, and then
ghoulishly dug up'. Shaw's experience had been the same. As he
explained in the chapters on education in *Everybody's Political What's
What*:

'My school was conducted on the assumption that knowledge of
Latin is still the be-all and the end-all of education. This was a matter
of course: I was given no reason why I should learn Latin instead of
some living language. There was, in fact, no reason, as there were
plenty of translations of all the classics that have any survival value.
The method of teaching was barbarous: I was ordered to learn the
declensions and conjugations and instalments of the vocabulary by
rote on pain of being caned or "kept in" after school hours if I failed
to reel off my paradigms without prompting. When I could do this,
which was easy enough to a child accustomed to pick up new words
and memorise them, Caesar's commentaries and Virgil's famous epic
were thrust into my hands, and without a word of explanation as to
what these old commentaries had to do with me, or why I should
concern myself laboriously about an ancient Trojan called Aeneas, I
was ordered to enter the lists against Dryden and extemporize translations of these works, failing in which I should, as before, be caned
or kept in.'

The Churches, dominant in the various schools in Ireland, were no
less powerful in English education. Sometimes the clerical authority
was grossly abused, as in the case of Rochester Cathedral Grammar
School, where the clergy were exposed as shameless thieves of the
endowments left long ago for the poor boys who were to benefit by
them both there and later at the Universities. The conduct of the
deans and canons which a courageous reformer called Whiston

brought to light in 1849 is staggering in its callous peculation.

At Oxford and Cambridge the Church of England had long imposed a sectarian test on entrants. Not only unbelievers were excluded from these Anglican enclaves but Dissenters too. In 1854 a Universities Act had been passed with a view to ending this intolerance. But in many colleges there was evasion of what the dons considered to be an improper invasion of their liberty to be illiberal. When a young man called C. P. Scott, later famous as the editor of *The Manchester Guardian,* was sent to Oxford in 1865 he was barred from two houses of his choice. His offence was to be a Unitarian. Corpus Christi College distinguished itself by admitting him. While the literature of the time could be a national asset and even a glory of Early Victorian England, its education was a disgrace.

Shaw in later life denounced the British public schools of which he had been spared any personal experience. Many of them were Early Victorian creations; commercial expansion and the enlargement of the professions, known as liberal but in fact conservative, had largely increased the middle class with its middling wealth and its ambitions for a loftier status. Not all its sons could get into the old foundations of Eton, Harrow, Winchester, Shrewsbury, and Rugby; there had to be premises for the overflow. So came the new establishments at Marlborough, Cheltenham, Clifton, and elsewhere. They preferred the name of college to that of school, since it seemed to confer a higher social rank and to lift them above the ancient grammar schools frequented by the sons of shopkeepers and despised by those who thought commerce degrading if it were only of the retailers' kind.

At Rugby Dr Thomas Arnold had endeavoured to rescue one of the old and famous (or infamous) schools from the barbarism and brutality which had been the eighteenth-century routine typified by the reign of the flagellant Dr Keate at Eton. Arnold, who had been schooled at Winchester and became a Fellow of Oriel at Oxford, had suffered from religious doubts but so far overcame them as to be a devoted Christian as well as a devoted believer in the wonder-working influence of Christianity on British character, at least in the middle and upper classes. 'A thorough English gentleman,' he wrote, 'Christian, manly, and enlightened, is a finer specimen of humanity than any other country, I believe, could furnish.' Appointed Head Master of Rugby at the early age of thirty-three, he reigned there for fifteen years, dying of angina pectoris at the age of forty-six.

Such was his achievement and reputation as a reformer that he may be thought of as the Grand Old Man of English middle-class education. He was, in fact, its young man, completely dedicated to his muscular Christianity (he did not lay aside or spare the rod), immensely industrious, and in the end defeated. Readers of *Tom Brown's Schooldays* by Thomas Hughes, who was at Rugby under Arnold, can hardly conclude that the Head Master had created a wholly 'enlightened' community, or rescued his school from the savages whom he had set out to replace with Christian gentlemen. The book appeared a year after Shaw's birth and was long popular.

There was in Arnold's Rugby more freedom in the use of leisure than was customary in such academies later on. Out of the classroom the boys could pursue natural history and botany in the country instead of being tied down by compulsory games. Lytton Strachey, in the essay on Arnold in his *Eminent Victorians,* quoted an old pupil of Arnold's who said that 'the boys at this period leaned strongly towards flowers'. 'The words,' added the biographer, 'have an odd look today.' Arnold did respect intellectual ability and gave high privilege to his Sixth Form. But the scope of the young mind was severely limited by concentration on Dr Blimber's dead languages. The classical routine, 'the grand old fortifying curriculum', of which Shaw became a reluctant serf in the Dublin of the eighteen-sixties, was not to be enlarged.

The irony of Arnold's career was the adoption in the new public schools, which made his Rugby their model, of a worship of athletics which he had not encouraged and of standards alien to his. The young Christian scholar of his ideal was elsewhere to become a worshipper of games and 'good form', resentful, as were his masters, of any new ideas and well equipped only to follow the conventional professions,

military and civil, in a conventional way, and often more con-
scientious than competent. The game of cricket became far more
important than Christianity and football was in itself a faith.

'The common English games,' wrote Bowen, a master at Harrow,
in 1884, 'are of indescribable value. Without any exaggeration, I
declare that in our whole system there is nothing which, in my
opinion, approaches them in value . . . There lives more soul in
honest play, believe me, than in half the hymn-books.' Bowen
composed his own songs of worship:

> God give us bases to guard and beleaguer,
> Games to play out, whether earnest or fun,
> Fights for the fearless and goals for the eager,
> Twenty and thirty and forty years on.

It was a forward-looking creed. The generations might pass, but
nothing was to change and the believers would in gratitude and piety

> Say how, honour and fame at stake,
> Somebody played for the old School's sake.

Arnold had never intended that. He had made his classical scholars
more important than his scorers of tries, goals, and centuries. Yet his
Rugby has been more remembered by the world for a new form of
football than for its output of Christian soldiers marching onward,
with their heads erect and also well stuffed with scholarship in dead
languages.

It is a reasonable surmise that, if George Carr Shaw had been a
prosperous member of the Irish Ascendancy and had sent his son to
be a boarder in an English public school, the young George Bernard
would have run away to the disgrace of the family, or died in misery.
It is unlikely that he would have conformed to Bowen's vision of the
superb Christian athlete who had learned that any deviation from the
norm was 'not cricket' and that his duty after leaving school was 'to
keep a straight bat in life'. Better suicide, he might have decided, than
an abdication of the mind and reverence for 'good form'.

There were occasionally to be found, and more were slowly to arrive, schools in which there was far less imposed discipline and far more stimulation of initiative and self-development. An example of that was Bruce Castle on the northern fringe of London. Rowland Hill, better remembered for his postal reforms and penny stamp, had there established an academy highly recommended by Dickens for its 'inducements to self-reliance and self-exertion'. (Yet Dickens sent one of his sons to the unreformed Eton College at Windsor and not to the reformers' paradise at Tottenham, an action which can be interpreted as an incidental snobbery in the life of one who vehemently denounced the ruling English families and the observance of caste.) But the Liberty Halls, another of which appears in the humane establishment of Dr Strong described in *David Copperfield,* were extremely rare and have never become common. There was no such place in Shaw's Dublin where long prevailed the bleak and brutal creed that children were the vessels of original sin, only to be brought to virtue by the severity of discipline which accompanied cramming their heads with unexplained facts.

Christ had said of the little ones that theirs was the kingdom of heaven; but this was kept out of mind by schoolmasters, with the parents consenting. It was one of those unfortunate indiscretions of which the New Testament, in their secret but strongly held opinion, contained far too many. If the men of affairs could keep the Bible out of business, why should they not do the same in the classroom? In any case there was the Old Testament to reassure them about their use of the rod. How salutary the counsel in the book of Proverbs! 'He that spareth the rod hateth his son: but he that loves him chasteneth him betimes.' 'Withhold not correction from the child: for if thou beatest with the rod, he shall not die.' The Thwackums, thus instructed about the cane as a life-preserver, might not know much or care much about the Mosaic law in general, but here was something to their purpose. They dared not denounce Jesus publicly, but privately they were convinced that Jehovah knew best.

That deity had a short way with disobedience even if the law-breakers seemed to be committing only trivial offences. In the book of Numbers it is written that a man was found gathering sticks on the Sabbath day: 'The Lord said unto Moses, "The man shall surely be put to death; all the congregation shall stone him." ' And stoned he was. Yet many Victorians believed that every word in both Testaments was directly inspired by God. In that case there was ample justification for regarding all those guilty of being young as the spawn of Satan and only redeemable by 'chastening betimes'.

But a change had been coming. Some poets had been so audacious as to proclaim the idea of original virtue implicit in Christ's saying about the children. It was a belief that had appeared in the odes and lyrics of the romantic school. The little ones piped songs of innocence for Blake: 'White as an angel is the English child.' The gloomy flagellants, if they ever heard of Blake, may also have heard that he saw angels in his London garden and so could be dismissed as one of the more ludicrous members of the lunatic fringe. Then there was Wordsworth who had greeted the coming of the French Revolution as a blissful dawn. Fortunately for British conservatism this dreamer amid his Lakes had calmed down with the years and as Poet Laureate he commendably gave offence to nobody. But he had been on Blake's side. He had acclaimed the Child of Joy, trailing clouds of glory as he comes from God who is our home: 'Heaven lies about us in our infancy.' The world might become a prison-house, but the victims are committed to the cells untainted by inherent, inevitable, pre-natal sinfulness.

Yet soon after this, Mrs Sherwood, authoress of *The Fairchild Family*, a work widely read and approved, was still giving the Puritan view of original sin an endorsement of now unbelievable gruesomeness. Her Mr Fairchild finds texts to prove to his children that the nature of man, after Adam, is utterly and entirely sinful. His six-year-old son obediently repeats, 'I know that in me, that in my flesh, dwelleth no good thing'. God and elder folk were seen by Mrs Sherwood as members of a holy alliance which seems to us to be unholy beyond words. A girl in the story was against parental orders admiring her new dress by candlelight in front of a mirror; it caught fire and she was burned to death. This was presented by the authoress as 'a warning to all children how they presume to disobey their parents'. Blake and Wordsworth had not penetrated far.

But in 1858, just within Shaw's lifetime, even a schoolmaster could put forward the romantic view of the angel-child. This was Frederick William Farrar, toughly educated at one public school and a master at two others, Marlborough and Harrow. He wrote a book, *Eric, or Little by Little,* which reached a huge public, was much admired, and was later derided as the nonsense of a sentimental parson who mixed tears with honey as his form of ink. In this 'Tale of Roslyn School' Eric begins life as an innocent. That he is corrupted by evil companions does not contradict the picture of original virtue. Wickedness abounds and the boys who brought disaster to Eric's life, if they ever trailed clouds of glory at birth, had shed them rapidly and effectively. There was 'Brigson, a forefront fighter in the Devil's battles who did much to ruin many an immortal soul, a boy with a deep, unfathomable flood of moral turpitude'. Brigson had replaced as Satan's protagonist at Roslyn one Ball who had been expelled for dirty talk. Eric, though horrified by Ball, had not dared to speak out and denounce him. Such timidity, in the face of a very bad time to come had he raised a protesting voice, does not seem a fatal fault of character. But so it proved. Little by little the moral collapse proceeded and Eric went forward to disgrace and death.

The dying child had come into Victorian fashion and Dickens had given Farrar a powerful lead into this vale of tears. But both, while writing with the uninhibited emotionalism so dear to readers at that time, were on the side of the little angels and virtually maintaining a view of life and of human nature that was odious to the Old Testament fanatics who were holding as tightly as could be to their grip on the schools. Shaw in boyhood did not confront Thwackum at his worst, but he was inevitably faced with some cruelty as well as much drudgery and with the belief that all boys were certainly hell-bent unless thrashed off the path leading to the bonfire and told that in 'chastening betimes' lay their only hope of salvation. They were to consider their life-giving stripes as a cause for gratitude and not for rebellion or even resentment.

Dr Arnold had his doubts about the nature of his charges at Rugby. 'My object,' he said, 'will be if possible to form Christian men, for Christian boys I can hardly hope to make.' That may have been spoken in a moment of sharp disappointment when some of his hopefuls had failed him. He stood half-way between the optimists and pessimists. So did Thackeray, who first called his Charterhouse Slaughterhouse, but was later in life to beam sentimentally at the little 'gown-boys' of Grey Friars. The times were ripening for Farrar's admission that Blake's angel-child was a human possibility and could be found even in the public schools. These had not lost the reputation bestowed on them by Henry Fielding who had called them 'the nurseries of all vice and immorality'. Roslyn's fault was to have all too few in the mould of Eric, a cherub when he started out in his career, ready with a blush and a tear at the very thought of depravity.

Shaw's writing on education can be found in his political books and in the very lengthy Preface to *Misalliance,* a play of 1910. But before that in *Man and Superman,* dated 1901–3, he had put the opinion of Blake into the mouth of John Tanner, that revolutionary member of the Idle Rich Class. It had been Shaw's reasonable complaint that authors when creating remarkable authors in their fictions provided no examples of their authorship. He himself would not be so evasive. So he added to his play *The Revolutionist's Handbook* in which Tanner's vehement denunciations of capitalist and bourgeois society are set out. Perhaps it is unfair to attribute to Shaw every word of Tanner's onslaught, since Tanner is a fictional figure, but in general Tanner's views are supported by Shaw elsewhere. 'The vilest abortionist is he who attempts to mould a child's character' was one of the Revolutionist's apothegms. What would Dr Arnold, not to mention the scourging Puritans, have thought of that?

Blake would have applauded. So too might Shakespeare, of whose thinking Shaw took so poor a view. For Shakespeare had his visions of the angel-child. Says Polixenes of boyhood in *The Winter's Tale*:

> We were as twinn'd lambs that did frisk i' the sun,
> And bleat the one at the other: what we changed
> Was innocence for innocence; we knew not
> The doctrine of ill-doing, no, nor dreamed
> That any did.

That was Eric's world, with no Ball and Brigson to propagate ill-doing. It was also the world of Shaw's ideas about education. Let the child be himself and find his way. He did not attack only the character-forming pedagogues: he thought the parents no less guilty.

In the nineteen-sixties, when young people were on the rampage and practising many stupid and wasteful forms of vandalism and violence, it was commonly complained that parents had abdicated and that there was no authority in the home as well as far too little discipline in the school. But the Victorian father was a formidable person, sometimes almost a self-appointed Jehovah in the home.

Shaw was a great admirer of Samuel Butler, and gladly admitted his great obligation to Butler's thought, especially in his criticism of Darwin and the concept of evolution as accidental and not purposive. Butler's description of boyhood in his novel *The Way of All Flesh* is known to be largely autobiographical and it presents a damning and terrifying picture of what is now called 'the father figure'. It has been argued that Butler maligned his parent, Canon Butler, but there are many books about Victorian family life which confirm the general picture of a domestic deity who dominated with the rod while assuming a divine omniscience about the proper ways of living. Piety and severity, even brutality, went together. The child was still the hell-bent limb of Satan. When the father in Butler's novel has thrashed his son for faulty pronunciation and left him screaming he says, 'And now, Christine, we will have the servants into prayers.' The Biblical passage chosen was that already mentioned; the servants were reminded of the stoning of the sinner who gathered sticks on the Sabbath.

Exaggeration may be here, but such a book as Sir Edmund Gosse's

Samuel Butler

Father and Son amplifies such portraiture. That volume was published in 1907, but Gosse was born in 1849 and so was describing an early Victorian childhood in an intensely Puritanical home. His father disliked all celebration of Christmas because the second syllable of the word had for him the contagion of Roman rites. When he discovered that a Christmas pudding was being prepared in his house he threw it in the fire to avoid domestic contamination. In some wealthy and spacious Victorian homes, where there were nurseries and schoolrooms, tutors and governesses, parents went about their professional and social lives with small concern for their children whom they saw only at occasional hours. Mrs Winifred Peck, the daughter of Bishop Knox, in her reminiscences of childhood in an Episcopal household recorded the almost complete isolation of the young family which, incidentally, turned out to be brilliant in scholarship and literature. In less important homes, with fewer rooms and less staff, the parents were naturally more present, both commanding and demanding. Shaw protested that parent worship was a pestilence to be crushed quite as much as any tyranny of the schoolmaster who made it his duty to form character and form it in one pattern alone. He felt that a father enthroned or a too dominant mother were autocrats who could do immense harm. It is true that he had not had to put up with any domestic domineering himself. Posterity can be grateful to George Carr Shaw for being negligent and to his wife Lucinda for her detachment; she was described by her son 'as a Bohemian anarchist with lady-like instincts'. Few English homes and perhaps not many Irish ones resembled his.

Shaw's writings on education abound in typical tirades. They are most enjoyable to read because they are written with such delight in invective and with such a mastery of combative prose. He punished his victims with his pen as heartily as his hated pedagogues had plied their canes. But he is rarely helpful in practical suggestion. While everything is found to be wrong, the right which should replace it is sketched in the vaguest generalities. The workaday problems of running a home and mixing kindness with firmness were unknown to him. He was never a parent with children on his hands, order to maintain, and careers to plan. It must occur to the reader that the outlook in his writing on this subject is predominantly masculine; he seems to be thinking far more of boys than of girls although the feminine sex is usually the more numerous. In this he was Victorian; when the principal career open to women was in the marriage-market there was naturally little concern about their book-learning. Likely husbands were unlikely to be attracted by blue stockings. Education for middle-class girls was directed to the teaching of 'accomplishments', either at school or by a governess in the home. Whether piano-playing was likely to be a profitable matrimonial asset may be doubted; but it was a usual part of the routine.

A change, however, was coming. The idea of an academy for young ladies where the subjects taught were similar to those in boys' schools was making progress. There was one noticeable development in Shaw's infancy when the famous Dorothea Beale became head-mistress of the Cheltenham Ladies College in 1858 at the age of twenty-seven. She set high standards of instruction and remained formidably and successfully at that post until her death in 1906. Her primness in matters of conduct would now be deemed excessive to the point of absurdity, but she had established the right of a girl to as good a general education as a boy and to continue it later at university. Girton College was established at Cambridge in 1873 and Somerville College at Oxford in 1879. The foundation of St Hilda's

Hall, now College, at Oxford was largely due to Miss Beale. Shaw probably thought that putting girls through much the same curricula as boys at school and then sending them on to the universities was wasting time and talent in both cases, since he had no regard for the studies pursued or the degrees won in such places. But mostly he wrote of the schoolboy, not the undergraduate.

He expressed only an occasional awareness that children can be wantonly mischievous; that did occur to him when in later life he was subject to a purposeless persecution. That took the form of pelting with pebbles by some boys who regarded an elderly man with a beard as a natural target at a time when beards were scarce and mocked with the silly cry of 'Beaver'. Fortunately the marksmanship was poor and persistence slight; his formidable presence was enough to awe and scatter what he called his 'lapidators'. But he had a reminder that the angel-child of the poets and romantic theorists can be a young devil in fact. He had sometimes seen at his own schools what torture by ragging a master may have to face and argued that the prevailing system made the teachers and the taught natural enemies. That was easy to say, but he burked the harsh realities of keeping the disorderly in order. The problem of establishing authority without tyranny and combining discipline with humanity is not solved simply by denouncing the inhuman.

He had never, one must conclude, visited a national school in a district where the pupils are as tough as their parents and where, as one who had worked in such a place told me, the boys brought their razor blades with them to a classroom which they regarded as their jungle. John Tanner dismissed schoolmastering as a profession suitable to those good for nothing else: 'He who can, does; he who cannot, teaches.' It is a stinging epigram, and, like most uncharitable generalizations, unfair. However, it has some further relevance to those who in other departments of life are more ready to criticize than to create.

The fact that so many of the prosperous despatched their young to boarding schools for three-quarters of the year inclined Shaw to regard teachers as people paid by parents to take their brats off their hands and thus permit some peace in the home. Their job was sullenly keeping their side of the contract for wretchedly inadequate rewards. While denying the competence of the profession he occasionally admitted its miseries. As he put it, every prisoner in a gaol imprisons a warder and the incarceration of the former puts a life of bondage on the latter. That the usher can be more than a turn-key is a fact he overlooked or refused to admit.

In the lengthy Preface to *Misalliance* Shaw demanded a Child's Magna Carta and left its clauses largely unspecified. To claim that a child should have 'a Right of Egress from unpleasant places and unpleasant company' is of no value unless there is some definition of where unpleasantness begins. Are teachers to have the same right and to be entitled to egress from any school-house where the pupils are disorderly and distinctly bad companions? There was Shavian insistence on public provision for the material and physical needs of the child, but these have been generously met in the Welfare State; a cruelly neglected child is now the parents' disgrace and not the fault of the education authority. To the supply of moral and even religious instruction Shaw gave firm support and he also maintained that there could be no ethical teaching if education were purely secular. This opinion would be strongly contradicted by the humanists of today who believe that sensible and considerate behaviour can be commended on grounds of reason without basing it on a miraculous divine revelation. Some of Shaw's views on this subject would have horrified the secularists and atheists whose company he kept happily enough during his early years in London.

Wherever you turn in that Preface and in *Everybody's Political What's What* there are signs of loose thinking amid the continual and compelling glow of lucid writing. One is reminded of a remark made by C. E. Montague in a critical article on Shavian drama. In this the talents of G.B.S. were likened to an express train which tears along sucking up the minds of playgoers or readers as though they were bits of straw or empty paper-bags until they are suddenly dropped later on. Certainly in all that he wrote about schooling there is the dynamic energy of a powerful locomotive. To be thus absorbed in that engine's wake, even if the drop follows and leaves the mind crumpled with doubts and confusions, makes stimulating travel while one is in full course of suction.

Always the attack is directed against what is plainly made to seem stupid and brutal without consideration of a changing world and always there seems to be some ignorance of new methods and much wider curricula than were to be found in the eighteen-sixties when Shaw was a reluctant Latinist. The public schools which he derided continued, with a few exceptions, to be much like those of Arnold and Brown. It is true that Dr Blimber's exhumation of dead languages was maintained on the classical side, but Shaw never stopped to consider the degree of their mortification. 'They are dead but they won't lie down' is a jest which has some application to Greek and Latin tongues. Shaw said that we can get anything of value in the classics from translations; he did not consider the extent to which a knowledge of Latin eases the learning of other languages and a proper comprehension of our own. Nor did he notice that the men of science continually turn to ancient Greece to find names for their inventions and that some instruction in Greek is a short-cut to understanding what scientists are talking about. There is no evidence that he insisted on calling a telephone a far-speaker or geography an earth-picture in order to shake off the curse of Blimberism.

It is true that specialization on classical subjects was carried to absurd lengths. I can say that with full experience of a most narrow education. From the age of fifteen, when I was deflected from elementary mathematics, French, and some smatterings of English history, to that of twenty-two, when I had finished with 'Greats' at Oxford, I was strictly confined, with the final exception of a little modern philosophy, to the literature and history of the Greeks and Romans during a period of roughly a thousand years. All other reading I had to do in my spare time which was little enough. I never had a science lesson in my life. Religion too was afflicted with this classicism in a way that was better calculated to produce a dull fatigue than a lively interest in or affection for the Faith. To be dragged through the Epistles of St Paul in Greek may add to one's knowledge of that language; it did not endear me to that apostle and his theological opinions. In short, when a recipient of that education was through with it, he had to start to educate himself.

The system worked if those put to it had the right kind of mind for it, a fair memory, and the ability to imitate ancient authors when doing compositions in their languages. That is to say, it led up a ladder of scholarships to a proficiency which offered an immediately available career in teaching the same subjects to a new generation of classical conscripts. It also opened the way to the higher grades of the Civil Service. Its constant exams necessitated the ability to think clearly and get one's knowledge on to paper rapidly, making the best of what one knew and carefully concealing what one did not. To be quick and lucid are valuable attainments, but as an introduction to the world of yesterday the system was poor enough and for the world of today it was ridiculous. It was a training essentially absorbent and did nothing to stimulate creative power. If Shaw had been subjected to this kind of mental discipline, he would have so resented it as to become a disgraceful failure in class. It is significant that the British writers showing strikingly original powers during the last sixty or eighty years were not thus classically confined. There might have been no Shaw, no Wells, no Lawrence if they had been.

But there have been great alterations and expansions and the 'grand, old, fortifying curriculum' has been admitted to be also something of a fossil. Shaw did not live to see the now vigorous insistence on more and more instruction in the sciences, more training in modern languages, and more encouragement of natural aptitudes and tastes. This is manifest in the number of subjects available and in the use of time not rigidly dictated by classroom periods in schools. Shaw overlooked the reforms that were already beginning and spreading. It has been recognized that 'an arts education' could and should include the practice of the arts. In many places these are conceived in a liberal spirit with the encouragement of invention and experiment. The absorption of ancient history and the mimicry of old styles of composition are much less enforced. But Shaw continued to censure the twentieth-century Georgians as though they were the Early Victorians of Arnold's Rugby.

Yet, when all charges have been brought against Shaw for cloudiness in practical suggestion and ignorance or neglect of the educational improvement which took place during the later years of his life, the hurtle of the express train through schools, colleges, and universities takes the reader for an unforgettable ride. 'But it is not our province, who only gather his works and give them to you, to praise him. It is yours that read him: and there we hope, to your divers capacities, you will find enough both to draw and hold you; for his wit can no more lie hid than it could be lost. Read him therefore, and again and again.' Thus Shakespeare's colleagues and editors, Heminge and Condell, introduced the First Folio. Their words may well be repeated about the hammer of bardolatry who was Bernard Shaw and they are applicable to the energy and persuasion of his style whatever the nature of his subject. None could have provided a better argument for self-education.

CHAPTER FIVE

Shaw and Women

IN Shaw's writing about sex woman is the dominant partner. Indeed partner may be called a wholly misleading word, so much is man made to seem a victim of complete domination. The male is visualized as the instrument employed by the female in her instinctive compliance with the Life Force, its demand for fertility, and its self-continuing process. The woman selects her mate: and he, though he may attempt to decide his own destiny, is overruled.

In holding this opinion Shaw maintained that he had the support of Shakespeare's plays since in them 'woman always takes the initiative'. He had to admit exceptions, such as the farcical courtship of the Shrew by Petruchio and such boy-meets-girl infatuations as that of Ferdinand and Miranda. But the adult feminine characters seriously drawn are claimed as good servants of the Life Force, hunting their husbands as Helena pursues Bertram without shame or surrender of her purpose in *All's Well That Ends Well*. Of this piece Shaw strongly approved because he could discover in it a favourable preview of the Ibsenite heroine and the unwomanly woman. Helena is as resolute in her seizure of a husband as is Ann Whitefield in her appropriation of John Tanner in *Man and Superman*. In the Preface to that piece Shaw stated that he could see women in no other way. 'I find in my own plays that Woman, projecting herself dramatically by my hands (a process over which, I assure you, I have no more real control than I have over my wife), behaves just as Woman did in the plays of Shakespear.'

Shaw's reasons for continuing to hold this opinion so strongly may have been based only on his objective study of the way of the world, but it is reasonable to suppose that he was also generalizing from his own experience. It is therefore important for an understanding and valuation of Shaw's thinking to know at least something of his relations with women from the time of his adolescence.

In his advice to Frank Harris on how to treat 'Sex in Biography', a letter preserved in *Sixteen Self-Sketches*, Shaw stated that he had had no 'adventures' of a sexual kind until he had reached the age of twenty-nine. This, with some cause, left Harris amazed and sceptical. All that G.B.S. could confess of his adolescence was the continual exercise of his imagination in visions of love, a curiously romantic start for the realist-to-be. His dreams of fair women made him see himself as an incorrigible philanderer in fancy, while remaining an escapist in practice, 'running away,' as he said, 'whenever the handkerchief was thrown to me.' He had reasons for being evasive. Poverty has its pride and the lover must feel abashed if he cannot pay the bill for even the most simple entertaining.

During his early years in London Shaw was living in extreme penury. His clothes were just the necessary coverings of his body and they were shabby and hard-worn; he could not look the part of a gallant nor could he play it as a host even of the most modest kind. Normal hospitality was impossible. When he had an extra penny or two to spend on a meal it went on a less scanty dish of herbs at the vegetarian Wheatsheaf Restaurant. As a companion for the evening he was, no doubt, an incomparable talker, as amusing as fluent, and especially loquacious when he was holding forth as a reformer of society and a man with a load of doctrine. But he had the sense to realize that his women friends, unless they were as ascetic and earnest as himself, would not welcome a mess of Wheatsheaf pottage any the more for being accompanied by a pot of Socialist message.

Never at that time, he said, and not until he was in his forties had he any idea of marriage. If this was made plain or firmly hinted to a feminine companion, it was neither encouraging nor flattering to the listener. Moreover, he put his political duties as a Socialist gospeller before the social pleasures. He later explained that the company of the other sex was in those years always secondary to a promised appearance on a platform and to participation in a debate. He was quite frank about that. So for a girl to know herself less attractive than the audience at a gathering of the Marxist Social Democratic Federation was not likely to satisfy feminine self-esteem.

Nor was it any better consolation for 'a date' avoided or postponed to know that the occasion preferred was a debate of the Zetetical Society whose eruditely Grecian name signified the questing minds of its truth-seeking members. It must seem extraordinary in our age of ubiquitous television with its unexacting pleasures and home-keeping allures that going out, and possibly quite a long way out, in order to sit on hard chairs in sombre halls was then a popular exercise with those who wanted to improve their minds first and the world after that. A lively speaker or a disputed cause was magnetic. Audiences, if not large, were plentiful and widely dispersed. Shaw, after a nervous start as a speaker to the Zeteticals, soon made himself master of the platform technique and was in constant demand as an orator. Since the speech-making was usually an evening exercise and there might be long or slow journeys to some of the meeting-places, the time for gallantry was so much limited as to make his admirers despair.

When at last he broke out or allowed himself to be pursued, as he thought of it, the affairs came rapidly and in variety. During Shaw's early thirties a new flow of soul swamped the previous feast of reason. This is not another life of G.B.S. and those curious to know of his affairs in detail can find a full account of *la vie amoureuse* in the comprehensive biography by St John Ervine which is based on a close friendship and many Shavian letters and conversations. The matter is also and more succinctly handled by Hesketh Pearson in his life of Shaw. To understand his theories about sex it is necessary to consider them in the light of this increasing experience with its mixture of raptures and embarrassments.

The sequence of infatuations began with Alice Lockett, a hospital

74

nurse; she and Eleanor Marx were workaday and wage-earning members of the enamoured group. The others had private means or were seeking and sometimes achieving careers in the arts. The office-going girl was not there to be met. The womanly woman was in the home and the unwomanly had few chances to earn a living by using her brains in a professional way. As portrayed in Shaw's second and partly autobiographical piece, *The Philanderer,* she could exist tolerably if she had means enough to join an equivalent of the Ibsen Club, where some of the play's action takes place. She could sit smoking and talking beside the bust of the Norwegian Master, discussing the splendours of free love and would add practice to theory if the suitably uninhibited and co-operative male could be found.

Most disturbing of his companions was a widow of some wealth, Mrs Jenny Patterson, who was partly, if not wholly, the model for Julia Craven in *The Philanderer.* In that piece the title-part of Charteris is mainly a self-sketch of the early Shaw and the physical skirmishing over his desired person between Julia and Grace Tranfield was admitted by him to be taken from an actual tussle in which Mrs Patterson was combating Florence Farr, an actress who also appealed to the poet W. B. Yeats. If Jenny did indeed resemble Julia she must have been as infuriating as she was attractive; for some time she was the Dark Lady in Shaw's life; she broke down his long-maintained virginity, an achievement in which Miss Farr seems to have shared. But the latter was tranquil compared with the tempestuous Jenny Patterson who first fascinated and finally exasperated Shaw beyond endurance. The portrait of Julia was his retort and a final one; he had escaped.

With these exceptions Shaw's affairs were platonic. He greatly admired and was admired by Mrs Annie Besant, a most effective public speaker who gratified him by becoming a Fabian Socialist when he least expected a conversion. She was a ready changer of her creeds, holding opinions passionately and dropping them easily. She first married and parted from a mild Anglican clergyman. Then she swerved to Bradlaugh's vehement atheism and ended in the alti-

Annie Besant   *Jenny Patterson*

tudes of theosophy. Like Shaw she could triumph on any platform. Their attachment remained innocently intellectual. It might not have done so since Mrs Besant had offered to live with him; it had to be 'in sin' since her parson husband was living and there had been no divorce. She presented Shaw with her contractual arrangements for a free-love partnership. He could discern no freedom for himself in these suggestions for a supposedly peaceful co-existence and decided that the terms were 'worse than all the vows of all the Churches on earth'. He would have none of that.

The Philanderer has never been liked and few, if any, will be able to see a revival on the stage in the future. But it is easily readable and has its own documentary value for those interested in Shaw's life when he was emerging from his lean and rather lonely years and entering the society of the unconventional and Bohemian types in late Victorian London. Ibsen, having denounced the posturing romantics who 'held up the banner of the Ideal', turned round in *The Wild Duck* to expose the harm that could be done by the relentless realist who must rob weaker folk of the dreams and illusions sustaining their lives. Shaw in the same way turned on his own progressive notions and friends and held himself up to by no means savage ridicule as Leonard Charteris. Leonard is the 'advanced' bachelor of the eighteen-nineties, both attractive and attracted. His pursuit of intellectual amours leads him into a whole thicket of trouble where the thorns are as plentiful as the roses and raptures. In his own summing up, 'The fickleness of the women I love is only equalled by the infernal constancy of the women who love me.' There spoke Shaw.

On the fringe of middle-class Socialism, with the Webbs at its austere centre, there was that juvenile devotion to novelty which is natural to the livelier members of every generation. 'Do you suppose it's a joke to be situated as I am?' says Charteris. 'You've got your head so stuffed with the New Humor and the New Woman and New This, That, and the Other all mixed up with your own Old Adam, that you've lost your senses.' Shaw, in whom the Old Adam was asserting himself, did not lose his senses but was put to some trouble to keep them. He did not fail in his self-imposed and unpaid labours as a Socialist propagandist while he had to keep up his workaday and ill-paid journalism. Further labour went to his letter-writing which was copious. That he could do so much was due to his astonishing capacity for work which always came before play. Ordinary amusements he hated and the kind of intellectual flirtation enjoyed by the Ibsenites was his only form of sport. He was in the up-to-date swim, which was amusing, but he had a battle to keep afloat when Jenny Patterson was splashing possessively about him on these sands of pleasure.

A larger and much more prominent cult in the early Shavian years was that of the Aesthetes. As early as 1881 W. S. Gilbert in the libretto of *Patience* had mocked South Kensington's affected medievalism, its preciosity, and curious attitudes. The fleshly poet Bunthorne has been generally taken to satirize Oscar Wilde who was then, at the age of twenty-five, making various kinds of name. But he was more up-to-date than antiquarian in his fashionable gambits and his chatter can hardly be called 'transcendental'. Shaw had various opinions of Wilde. As an Irishman he called him 'a prime specimen of the sort of fellow-townsman I most loathe; to wit, the Dublin snob'. But he could enjoy his company, with wit matched against wit, and was glad to meet him in Chelsea wearing clothes similar to his own, a soft hat and a tweed suit. His impression of Wilde is far apart from the Bunthorne model, a creature of 'languid spleen' who 'walked down Piccadilly with a poppy or a lily in his medieval hand', afflicted with platonic affections for vegetable loves. Wilde might be called a fleshly poet, but his carnality was wholly different from Bunthorne's.

What was wholly detestable to Shaw was the playboy pessimism of the *fin-de-siècle* café poets and the juvenile delight in the macabre. The sinister sensuality, so brilliantly limned by Aubrey Beardsley, had no attraction for the serious and Socialist Shaw, crusading and pamphleteering for the regeneration of capitalist society and more addicted to studying a Blue Book than to poring over the *Yellow Book* in which the aestheticism of the eighteen-nineties was mingled with some work of quite different quality. Wilde had asserted that all art, or at least all good art, is entirely useless. Shaw demanded that art should always be didactic, serving a social purpose. Both statements are so extreme as to be untenable, but naturally such contrasted creeds could not be reconciled. Nora of *The Doll's House* banged the door and walked out to be a free and independent woman of the Shavian ideal. She would have bored Wilde beyond words, if Oscar was ever at a loss for words. The author of *Salome* and *The Picture of Dorian Gray* would not have been at home in any Ibsen Club.

Oscar Wilde
in his youth

Shaw had no sympathy with a general cynicism; particular cynicisms, about democracy and politicians, for example, were, he thought, justified by the facts of public life; but a sweeping pessimism about the world in general was repulsive to the vitalist philosophy of creative evolution. To be part of a purpose, to work for it until exhausted, to 'plod on and keep the passion fresh' (especially the intellectual passion) was his idea of a satisfying existence. 'I no longer desire happiness; life is nobler than that.' Such Puritanism in its highest form was as intolerant of the aesthetes' yawning self-indulgence in the pleasures of the moment as of a cult of art for artistry's sake.

Wilde's trial and conviction have put a stamp of homosexuality on the eighteen-nineties, a period in which it was probably less common than it is now and certainly could not be flaunted. It was not a subject mentionable in the theatre then; now its addicts swarm in our plays and books and sometimes give the impression that only the abnormal are normal. Shaw would have given the subject stage treatment, Censor or no Censor, if he had wanted to. But he kept it out of his themes and characterizations. Humanely he viewed the possession of such tendencies as a misfortune. In the Preface to *The Dark Lady of the Sonnets* he wrote of 'the most cruel and pitiable of all freaks of nature, the freak which transposes the normal aim of the affections'. He said this in 1910, long before the present obsession with homosexuality, but he knew that a change was coming, since he added that when he was a boy every well-known man was accused of beating his wife. 'Later on,' Shaw added, 'he was accused of psychopathic derangement.' He neither excused Wilde nor approved of a prolonged persecution when his severe punishment was over. The British in a mood of self-righteousness were odious to him.

'Ladies whose bright eyes rain influence' did not make their impact on G.B.S. with beauty alone. There had to be persuasion of the mind as well. He had frequent sessions with Mrs Hubert Bland who, using her unmarried name of E. Nesbit, became and long remained a very popular writer of children's stories. Her errant husband, picturesque, flamboyant, and an incongruous member of this Socialist group which included many serious and some dedicated types, found one partnership insufficient for his needs. His official wife had ample justification in playing hostess to the philanderer: but this indulgence, though powerful enough to make Shaw miss his last train more than once and tramp the whole way from Blackheath to London, was a blameless diversion. He declared that none of his friendships with women whose husbands were alive was of an adulterous kind.

There was also May Morris, whose father, William, made his Hammersmith home a centre of Socialist meetings. Morris was impelled towards Socialism as much by the ugliness as by the economic conditions of capitalist society. His reforms of English taste in furnishings, wallpaper, and printing were more effective than his approaches to the working-class, whose home life was so different from his own. A failure in political doctrine, he prevailed in domestic décor. Shaw, as his guest, met perfect cooking and a style of living to which he was a stranger. May Morris was one of the notable decorations of her father's riverside house and Shaw was immediately smitten when he saw her. But for once he was struck more speechless than eloquent. He remained silent about the admiration which she inspired. This was of a curiously elevated kind. It was not impressed on her that Shaw was thinking of 'a Mystical Betrothal', an odd phrase to come from the unromantic Ibsenite. Later, having received no intimation of these surging emotions, she betrothed herself to a man of no consequence. The marriage failed.

Another friendship was with Eleanor, a daughter of Karl Marx. She was one of Shaw's associates in the reading-room of the British Museum. She was a good linguist and could make a living as a capable translator. (When re-reading an English version of Flaubert's *Madame Bovary*, I noticed that it was Eleanor's work and good work, too.) She was in demand amid the babel of international Socialist congresses. This affair seems never to have gone far. 'Fairly cordial' is Hesketh Pearson's description of it. Eleanor lived for a while with a doctor of science, Edward Aveling, whose principal achievement was a scientific application to borrowing money which he had no intention of repaying; a coaxing charm was his substitute for lack of conscience. He collected women as airily as he collected cash. When his wife died and Eleanor expected him to marry her, he dropped her and she later committed suicide. Yet Shaw maintained that amid all his duplicity Aveling was completely staunch in his opinions; girls and creditors he would betray, Socialism and atheism never. This unscrupulous but plausible rogue has been given an abiding portrait as Louis Dubedat in *The Doctor's Dilemma* and so has received more immortality than he merited.

Eleanor might be described as a congress-comrade at a time when Socialists were often in conference and briskly quarrelling. If there was affection, it was mixed with doctrinal disputation. Quite different were the friendships of the theatre which had little or no political element. With Janet Achurch, a prominent actress of the Ibsenite school and the first woman to play the part of Candida, Shaw corresponded at length. He wrote even more assiduously to Ellen Terry. The amount of time and energy which he gave all his life to letter-writing is amazing. He poured forth postcards to myriads who had no reason to expect an answer and sent despatches of great length and typical cogency to his friends and colleagues and sometimes to those who hardly knew him. These activities were completely disinterested since he frequently put into his epistles long statements of opinion which were really saleable articles, and this he continued to do even when his work commanded soaring prices. On Ellen Terry he bestowed professional advice as well as personal admiration, but she could hold her own in argument about the theatre of the time, her performances, and her place in it. They never met while he was a practising dramatic critic but he continued to be her unwearying correspondent. She could not be called one of the women in his life: but she was a presence, almost a goddess, in the background.

Much closer contact was established later on by Mrs Patrick Campbell. This wayward beauty could act with devastating power

*Mrs Patrick
Campbell*

when she chose; but she did not always choose to do so. With a fiery and capricious temper, a rare wit, and a biting tongue, she became the tigress of the English stage in the eighteen-nineties and remained a character as baffling to her fellow players as she could be brilliant when on her good behaviour. She was fascinated by Shaw, set out to capture him, called him Joey her clown, and to some extent fascinated him. Like Jenny Patterson, she was even ready for physical violence in the lists of love. Like Jenny, she was punished in a play. The ridiculous grapple of King Magnus and Orinthia in *The Apple Cart,* produced in 1929, is based on some memories of in-fighting when Shaw was insisting on leaving Mrs Pat's company for home and duty. Fifteen years earlier she had played the leading part of Shaw's Eliza Doolittle in *Pygmalion,* the piece which was later to capture the world in musical form as *My Fair Lady*. In the rehearsing and performance of *Pygmalion* Mrs Pat drove both Shaw and the actor-manager Beerbohm Tree to distraction. As an intruder in the

82

dramatist's life she had greatly distressed Charlotte Shaw and wasted a great man's time when he was in the fullness of his power. She pestered him with some success but did not achieve the kind of conquest she wanted.

Charlotte Payne-Townshend has already been encountered among some sporting company and a little serious politics in the survey of Shaw's Ireland. After her father's death she left that country in order to see more of the world. She was tired of the frivolities of her Ascendancy associates and of the routines of the Anglo-Irish life into which she could have married had she chosen. She greatly enjoyed travel and now had the freedom and the funds to enjoy it. Shaw, when he first met and became friendly with her, spoke of his 'green-eyed millionairess'; she was by no means that, but an income of some thousands a year with the purchasing power of the pound in the eighteen-nineties enabled her to be a benefactress as well as to live where and how she pleased. She liked trains, ships, hotels, and was much on the move, since she was eager to see historically important places. She also hoped to meet, in London and abroad, the intellectually important people of the day.

In Rome she had encountered the Swedish doctor Axel Munthe, later famous and enriched as the author of *The Story of San Michele*. He was then making a reputation as a physician and was praised for being fearless and capable in coping with dangerous epidemics. He was also a clever talker with a magnetic personality, becoming popular and even lionized wherever he went. An acquaintance with Charlotte ripened. She with her unconventional kind of beauty had her attractive moments; with her modesty and courtesy she was an attentive and even devoted listener to a man who so much liked an audience and throve on admiration. Here for her was the entry to a new world of distinguished company and fresh ideas. She may be said to have lost her heart—or part of it. But Munthe, ambitious and climbing, was not losing anything on his way up. The affair came to nothing and Charlotte came to London.

Here, in 1896, there were even more important and exciting people to be met than in Rome or Capri. Here was a man of forty (almost her own age) called Bernard Shaw who combined a name for devastating brilliance in journalism and conversation with addiction to left-wing politics. Charlotte was anxious to escape from the conventional society of her Irish friends and relations, was not terrified by the mention of Socialism, and was ready to help as well as to mix with the leaders of progressive causes. She joined with enthusiasm in the campaign for women's rights and she was open to radical ideas of all kinds. She was taken up by Sidney and Beatrice Webb of the Fabian Society as an interesting recruit whose appeal to them was all the greater because she had money and was ready to spend it on suitable causes for which they needed support. Since Shaw was so closely associated with the Webbs, it was inevitable that she should soon meet Socialism's 'bold, unbiddable boy'.

This first occurred at the Webbs' London house in January, 1896. But it was not until late in that summer that the couple saw much of each other. A closer association was made in a country rectory near Saxmundham in Suffolk. The Webbs' habit was to rent furnished houses and gather appropriate political company in August. Rectories were not luxurious but they could be cheap as well as spacious. The Fabians were not there to be cosseted and were not expected to feast and lounge through a month of lush vacation. The Webbs, busy with their books, brought their files and papers; those whom they assembled had work of their own in mind or on hand.

The light relief for those who did not want to read or write all day, as the Webbs usually did, was bicycling in the afternoon to stretch the limbs followed by some light exercise for the mind at night in discussion of all kinds of topics. Shaw and Charlotte, leaving the sterner spirits to their Reports and Blue Books, pedalled through the East Anglian lanes which were agreeably free of exhausting hills. They took their part (he presumably a leading part) in the nocturnal palaver. Beatrice Webb, a constant diarist, recorded of this summer that 'Charlotte and G.B.S. have been scouring the country together and have been sitting up late at night. To all seeming she is in love with the brilliant Philanderer and he is taken in his cold sort of way'.

This reference to a woman in love and a man somewhat reluctantly 'taken' might seem to imply that the devouring woman about whom Shaw theorized was in fact at work in Suffolk and preparing to pounce. That he continued to dramatize the dominant and triumphant husband-snatcher after his marriage may also be taken as a sign that, when he became friendly with Charlotte, he felt himself to be as much doomed as is John Tanner when Ann Whitefield sets about him in the fourth act of *Man and Superman*. This is completely disproved by the facts.

A woman on the pounce does not wait two years before she takes action and Charlotte was not a pouncing type. For years avoiding marriage and disliking the very thought of its physical aspect, she now became an interested admirer of Shaw, invited him to join company at her flat in Adelphi Terrace, and gradually helped an overworked man to escape some of his pressures and sort out some of his correspondence; she also did some typing for him. They were together in August, 1897, when the Webbs took a house in Wales in order to work on their history of trade unionism. Shaw was preparing his plays for publication in book form and Charlotte was ready to assist. Mrs Webb recorded that 'he persuades himself that by keeping her occupied he is doing her good'. Things might have gone on like that for years; he was still putting the idea of marriage with anybody out of mind and she was still contentedly acting as an unpaid secretary, a service agreeable to both. The age of romance and of possible maternity for her was nearly over. When they did go to the Registrar in the following June he was forty-two and she was forty-one. Also the decision to marry was provoked by an accident.

It might be said that Charlotte did at last pounce. But she did so as a nurse, almost as a mother. In so far as she brought a very sick man back to health she could be called a servant of the Life Force which Shaw thought to be so powerfully operative in the nature of women and the relations of the sexes. But the Life Force as the agent of fertility had nothing whatever to do with the resort to matrimony in this case. Bourgeois respectability, not surging sexuality, was the cause of a certificated union registered in the presence of two Fabian friends of G.B.S., Graham Wallas and Henry Stephen Salt, and probably, though this is not certain, never consummated.

Janet Dunbar, in her life of Mrs G.B.S., describes as 'ludicrously wide of the facts' the gossips' account of Shaw being snatched helpless to a country house where he offered marriage to avoid a scandal. What did settle the matter was Charlotte's realization that Shaw was getting very lame, was in great pain, was in real danger of collapse, was incapable of looking after himself, and was getting no proper care from his mother and sister in Fitzroy Square. There it was the domestic policy to leave the man of the house alone, which was agreeable to G.B.S. But, thus liberated in one way, he was drudging for very long hours in a small study never properly tidied and was feeding on scrappy and occasional meals. Charlotte came, saw, and resolved that rescue was essential. The poison in the foot might spread, and he was still trying to go to his theatres and carry on with his work. He must be got away for a complete rest and proper nursing. Having rented a house in the good hill air near Hindhead, she arranged and he agreed to a hasty wedding in London as the simplest way of settling down quietly, stopping talk, and achieving a most necessary cure.

The marriage was peaceful and in one way fruitful. Although Charlotte would not, and perhaps at her age could not, have a child, it was as a married man that Shaw came to the summit of his achievement and to his greatest fertility of output in writing of all kinds. She could feel that she was the midwife of his principal progeny. She could also feel that she had found the essential purpose of her life; but she was careful never to overplay the role of a guardian-wife. She stood back and did not interfere with his delight in publicity which she herself hated. Shrewdly she left him to work out his own ideas, not trying to be his intellectual equal. She had her own social interests and her own considerable sagacity; she had a vein of mysticism and various types of Higher Thought appealed to her from time to time;

Charlotte Shaw

into those hazy altitudes G.B.S. preferred not to wander. Their mutual understanding made for a usually serene as well as abiding attachment. It could not be a marriage of similar minds; instead it was a union of congenial and considerate personalities.

There were some rifts. She retained her love of travel and he could not shed his dislike of it. He soon wearied of packing up and moving on and of long voyages at sea. When he was established as a Great Man, a status quite acceptable to him, Charlotte increasingly felt that he must be kept from overworking and be relieved of the social stresses and continual invitations and interruptions of a career so much discussed and with its privacy so frequently menaced. So he became a reluctant globe-trotter and there were dissensions over the long escapes from England which she enjoyed as well as advocated. His idea of rustication for the sake of peace and quiet was retreat to the rather commonplace country house at Ayot St Lawrence quite close to London which he retained till the end of his life. Charlotte found it dull at times; but his study and the garden, when the weather allowed, were his favourite workshops for nearly fifty years.

There was minor trouble with invasive feminine admirers, some of whom had to be sharply put off the premises, and there was a major distress for Charlotte when Mrs Patrick Campbell was pursuing her Joey with as little scruple as reserve. But the union which had been caused by an illness and might never have been made without it was as felicitous as any partnership with such a man as G.B.S. could be. The rule that Socialists are the greatest individualists was amply exemplified in his life. He had his vanities and caprices. He liked to sustain in public the character part which he created in his early years of the irrepressible and even brassy G.B.S. Below that false but entertaining surface was the shy, kindly, and generous Bernard Shaw 'known to his own'. Of that perceptive company Charlotte was naturally the first and closest member.

It is plain from the facts of Shaw's life that his theory of woman as a man-hunter and determined maker of marriages owed nothing to his early life when he saw so little of the other sex. Some theorizing may have come from his contacts with the unwomanly women whom he met in his thirties when Ibsenism was in the air. Taught by his friends in this climate not 'to run away when the handkerchief was thrown' he could decide that the Life Force was a great propeller of such small linen. But his marriage to Charlotte gave no support to the notions which he retained in his writing. On the verge of a breakdown he had been delivered not devoured. His debt to his wife was large, but it did not include a model for Ann Whitefield.

CHAPTER SIX

Woman's Place

THE careers open to women of his own class and of wealthier families during Shaw's youth in Dublin and his early years in London were narrowly confined. The principal occupation was marriage. For the daughter of a wealthy or moderately prosperous family that was the expected and often the only prospect. Her business and that of her contriving mother was to find a husband of satisfactory income and approved status. If some romantic attachment were included that was an agreeable but not essential addition to the marriage settlement. This was the procedure often depicted in the richer households in many Victorian novels. It was also an aristocratic tradition: the unions of the nobility had long been property deals.

Contrasted with this cynical view of match-making in the Vanity Fairs of the cities and the Horseback Halls of the countryside, there was an abundance of sentimental fiction written for the popular market with the assumption that a peal of wedding bells inevitably rang in years of felicity to come. The Brownings attained in practice, as well as commended in their poetry, a Christian idealism in courtship and wedlock, a partnership both passionate and pure. They had their admirers, but matrimony as encountered in the work of Dickens and Thackeray is more of a convenient economic arrangement than the product of a lyric love. Among the advantages of the system was the saving of bourgeois homes from overcrowding by unoccupied daughters with a wearisome quantity of time on their hands.

These young women, if unable to fill their days while waiting for the suitable match, could undertake a few genteel activities since their education was supposed to provide them with the requisite accomplishments. They had their music and their needlework, but there was no thought of seeking regular employment and of using professionally what brains and qualifications they might possess. When we are faced with Shaw's often repeated assertion that woman always and actively takes the initiative in matrimonial arrangements, we must remember the kind of upper- and middle-class society which, though he was out of it himself as a youngster, he was meeting in books. In it the girls had to be saleswomen; if they could not put themselves effectively on the counter, they would remain, as the callous put it, 'on the shelf'. Shaw's disgust with that necessity of the single woman continued to shape his opinions about women's rights.

For the children of the poor there was in the industrial areas plenty of work from which the girls were not excluded. There was also a vast demand for domestic servants; the size of the indoor staffs of which we read in the memoirs of the time must seem incredible to the members of the middle class today. The town house still stands in all its gaunt inconvenience as the evidence of a society in which cheap and abundant labour was taken for granted. Many of these mansions have been split into four or five flats or maisonettes of a not very comfortable kind. In mid-Victorian England comfort could only be got if there were numerous maids to carry coals and hot water up the interminable stairs, to sweep and dust on a grand scale, and to carry ample meals from basement kitchens. The labours of these drudges were supervised, at least in the more prosperous homes, by formidable feminine housekeepers and menservants who had no need to risk their dignity by becoming noticeably mobile.

In the country houses (some not of the wealthiest kind) described by Jane Austen at the beginning of the nineteenth century, the capable and copious supply of servants is always presumed to be there. There is much ado in finding husbands, none in finding maids. The 'staff problem' simply does not arise. It is remarkable that an authoress so perceptive in her treatment of the possessing class was so little interested in those who worked in their homes. The dilemmas and sufferings of the servants' hall must have been there, but they do not receive the delicate sympathy bestowed on Miss Austen's heroines. We must go to Dickens to meet the footmen and the 'slavey'.

Now there is so much work to be done in commerce and industry, such insistence on continual increase of output, and so vigorous a demand for the labour of both sexes that we may be surprised to find Victorian society economically viable while myriads of hands were deflected to domestic service. Any family with social ranking of the humblest kind had to keep a resident maid in order not to be disgraced. As the income rose, the staff had to rise with it. Then the quantity of servants was the symbol of status; the price of the motor-car now helps to settle social ranking in homes where the wife and mother gets little, if any, hired help. That the parents of G.B.S., though finding it hard to pay their way, had a 'thorough-servant' living in the basement and working for eight pounds a year has already been mentioned. Even up till 1914 huge homes were still being built in cities and on country estates which were habitable by those planning to dwell in these monstrous places only if there were a certainty of obtaining servants by the score.

The mistress of a quite prosperous home is now the stay-at-home drudge. Her daughters go out to earn wages or salaries and make their spare time a good time. Shaw's indignation at the neglect of young women's capacities and the humiliations of the marriage-market is now completely out-of-date. Today if they have energy and ability they can go almost anywhere and practise almost any profession. (The exceptions to this latitude of admission are peculiar. They include priesthood in the Roman Catholic and Anglican Churches and the holding of a licence for training race-horses.) Even if the parents can afford to have a daughter at home she is unlikely to want to stay there. She much prefers to be out and about and earning, even if going to a London job means hours of overcrowded and exhausting travel. The contrast with mid-Victorian England is immense. Woman's place, as most men saw it then, continued to be the home. Many professions were still masculine preserves jealously guarded; business life was not to be invaded by feminine trespassers. Had there been attractive young women sharing the desks in the Dublin offices and banks while Shaw was a clerk and cashier in a land-agency, he might not have been such a late developer in matters of feminine friendships.

What could the unmarried daughter of a respectable but indigent family do within the limits of accepted custom? She could teach in a school or be a governess to a family. The Brontë sisters had their turn of this way of life; it provided a bed, probably hard, and board, far from luxurious, and a salary that would do little more than clothe them meagrely. Whether the position of a governess was agreeable or at least tolerable depended on the attitude of her employers. They might be cold and aloof or, if she were lucky, friendly and considerate: generally she inhabited a social mezzanine floor, well above the below-stairs life of the domestic servants, but not on the level of her employers' drawing-room. She was almost a lady teaching others to be wholly lady-like. She could hope for an ultimate escape by marriage, but the opportunities for meeting eligible men were scanty. She might grow old as a spinster or become a dragon resembling that Mrs General of 'prunes and prisms' fame whom Mr Dorrit engaged to educate his daughter Fanny. The governess might not be respected by her employers but she was never less than respectable in the eyes of the world.

Shaw's mother, who had to earn money, taught singing and did so competently both in Dublin and London. To have vocalists frequently under instruction in a small home is unlikely to make it easily habitable by others. It is natural to imagine that George Carr Shaw's regular outings in search of the social glass may have been prompted by the efforts of his wife's pupils. But G.B.S. does not appear to have complained.

While business did not welcome women, the arts had to open the doors to feminine performers. Even a lady could sing for her supper. Shaw's elder sister Lucy joined the Carl Rosa Opera Company and rose high enough to take the leading part in the very popular piece called *Dorothy*; in this role she was seen and heard by her critical brother who found her performance 'all the more desperately vapid because she suggested artistic gifts wasting in complete abeyance'. That was a notice unlikely to gratify its victim; but at least the possession of gifts was admitted. Shaw's other sister, Elinor Agnes, was an invalid and died so young that there was no employment problem in her case.

Women could go on the stage or mount the teacher's dais; it was not considered unwomanly to live by the pen. Rather lonely beginnings in novel-writing had been made by Fanny Burney and Jane Austen. The middle of the nineteenth century was rich in woman novelists. The Brontës were not the only pioneers who came out of the parsonage. There was Elizabeth Cleghorn, the daughter of one Unitarian minister and married to another. As Mrs Gaskell she won a justified recognition with her story *Mary Barton*. In this book she forcibly reminded the comfortable reader of uncomfortable working-class lives. Five years later in *Cranford* she turned with even more success to a gently humorous picture of her own class in her own place, the quiet country town of Knutsford in Cheshire. Her sympathetic life of Charlotte Brontë followed and she continued to be a much-read novelist.

There could be a place, too, though this was uncommon, in the more serious kind of journalism. Mary Ann Evans, the daughter of a Midland land-agent, brought up in a Puritan atmosphere, broke away from her faith and her family and was able to make a living on the fringe of Fleet Street before she became, under the pseudonym of George Eliot, a novelist of high reputation with a large readership. At the age of thirty-two she was assistant editor of the *Westminster Review*. Her fiction began in 1858 with *Scenes of Clerical Life,* which was rapidly followed by *Adam Bede, The Mill on the Floss,* and *Silas Marner.* Her work was then expected to have such a reception that, while Thackeray was editing the *Cornhill Review,* she was offered ten thousand pounds for the serial and book rights of her new story in hand. This was *Romola,* which appeared, and disappointed, in 1863.

George Eliot

Considering the purchasing power of money and the trifling rate of income tax, that was an enormous sum. Naturally there was a considerable feminine entry to the profession and fiction was soon to provide some profitable careers for women. But chances of victory in that field are inevitably limited. It is arable land easily over-cropped. A host of authors cannot live by taking in each other's novels.

Poor women were much in demand for factory labour as well as for the numerous posts 'below stairs' in domestic service. A long series of unexacting and not always implemented Factory Acts did, during the nineteenth century, mitigate to some extent the appalling conditions of life in the mills after the Industrial Revolution. But official inspection was too weak and too occasional to keep up with the shameless employer. Work carried on in small premises, as was much of the clothing trade, remained sweated labour at its worst. Thomas Hood had denounced the virtual enslavement of the seamstress in *The Song of the Shirt,* which appeared in *Punch* in 1843. If public opinion was shocked, reform was not the result. Shaw maintained in *The Millionairess,* a play whose action is dated in 1935, that the pay in what is known as the Rag Trade was still abominable. The squalor and poverty of the Shirt-Song were still there.

In this piece the wealthy, omni-competent Epifania, a born feminine organizer and gifted member of 'the boss class', investigates the East End basement of a clothier and tells him how to run his business to better advantage for all concerned. While she is first questioning him she is told that a woman's 'natural wage' is 'tuppence ha'penny an hour' for a twelve-hour day. The man's wife backs him up with the remark that a good worker can thus earn twelve to fifteen shillings a week in a match-factory 'which was a godsend to my mother'. Shaw also made the point that when the British government urged the women of Britain to do their bit practically in 1914 and sew shirts for the huge influx of new soldiers, the rewards were still on the old Victorian level.

During most of Shaw's life the phrase 'sweated labour' was commonly in the news. Its particular plague-spot was, as he pointed out, the clothing industry and the East End of London was notorious for its 'sweat-shops'. Efforts to improve conditions by legislation and by the setting up of wages boards in the industries most notorious for exploitation, especially of women workers, achieved something. But a greater change could come only when women, instead of jostling each other in a scramble for jobs, were eagerly sought by jostling employers. The age of full (or nearly full) employment, once unimaginable as a normal feature of British life and especially so during the slump of 1931, had arrived with the war in 1939. This created a nation-wide demand for labour that did not vanish with the peace. The winds of change, when operative in financial inflation, wafted in the so-called age of affluence; the new prosperity could be called a fraud because, as more money went into circulation, the less it seemed to buy. But money did steadily flow and by 1964 the average wage of a male manual worker in England was over seventeen pounds a week. The women, it is true, were only averaging a little more than half that, but many of them who worked in offices were getting more and those holding responsible positions much more. At the same time the hours of work were shortened and the five-day week was fairly general.

Thus by the time of Shaw's death a paradoxical situation had been reached. The supposedly sheltered woman who as a housewife and mother stayed at home had become the least protected. She had no fixed hours or scale of remuneration while she coped with every kind of domestic care. The unmarried woman who went out to work to be, as Shaw was still thinking, an oppressed victim of the capitalist system, was now profiting by the scarcity value of her labour and could keep pace with inflation by demanding and insisting on getting more and more for her services. If anyone could be called sheltered it was the 'business girl' at large in a world once thought to be so cruel. 'Sweated labour' was in the home.

Another point to be considered is the relation between money and morals. It was Shaw's opinion (and one held by Dickens and many Radical and Socialist theorists and politicians) that poverty, not depravity, is the parent of vice and crime. With the spectacle of proletarian wage-slavery amid the rack-renting of slum property described by Shaw in *Widowers' Houses,* it seemed obvious to the reformers that here lay the cause of law-breaking and corruption of character. Shaw was convinced and definitely stated that no normal woman would endure the life of a prostitute if she could sell her labour at a fair wage in a decent occupation instead of selling her person in a degrading one. He may have been right when he said that because the woman's wage was often so low. But he was certainly proved by later experience to be wrong.

During the decade and a half following his death the search for workers rather than for work continued. Except in a few of the less prosperous areas, the national and local newspapers were carrying far more advertisements of situations vacant than of applications for work. There were incessant demands for all kinds of feminine labour

Women in industry—hatting factory in Manchester, 1909

including some highly paid positions. The competition of staff-seeking employers compelled the wages and salaries offered to be adequate and often ample. A girl could be reasonably paid while being trained for a business job and, when trained, could move upwards or to another better paid job elsewhere if she chose. But there were plenty who preferred to hear and receive another kind of call in another way of life. Prostitution, though driven off its old market in the streets by new legislation, continued to thrive in a thinly disguised seclusion.

Nor did availability of reasonably paid work put an end to picking and stealing with violence added, as it should have done according to the Shavian theory. Assault and robbery rose while the figures of unemployment dropped. The men who coshed night-watchmen and drove up in fast cars to rob a bank or a cashier carrying wages were not desperate for a crust of bread. It was no urgent compulsion of bitter need that caused the looting from railways of goods to the value of a million and a half pounds in a single year, which was the loss reported in 1964. Any store-manager or shopkeeper could tell of continual depredations by shoplifters, many of them women who were not in want at all.

The Prime Minister could have added to his statement of 1959 that the British people had never had it so good a later comment that they were never stealing so much. Convictions for shoplifting rose from an average of 23,000 during the years 1950–4 to nearly 53,000 in 1962. Self-service stores were then expecting to lose one per cent of their turnover to thieves. Convictions for thefts from houses were nearly doubled between 1950 and 1962, the figure soaring up from 18,500 to 33,600. Robbing of slot machines and meters trebled in the same period.

Thus the Shavian view of crime, which had been common among Radicals and Socialists, was proved to be an illusion. It was not the pauper seeking to be less poor but the newly affluent seeking to be more affluent who were defeating the efforts of an under-staffed police force and making the job of a bank clerk or a jeweller one of the dangerous trades. Mrs Warren had said in the play about her profession of manageress and shareholder in private hotels which were really elegant brothels that 'the only way for a woman to provide for herself decently is to be good to some man that can afford to be good to her'. Those conditions had been left far behind during Shaw's lifetime. The girls employed by Mrs Warren had an abundance of other occupations available.

Shaw admitted in the same play, on which he was working in 1893, that a new woman was already arriving, one who was determined to make a decent living without angling for a husband or otherwise selling her charms. She could now do so because at last a few professional opportunities were becoming open to women. Such was Mrs Warren's daughter, Vivie. Revolted by the discovery of her mother's hidden and profitable life, she took work as an actuary in an office in Chancery Lane and set out to study law as well.

But Vivie was an exceptional person. Mrs Warren had done far more for her daughter than many a respectable and wealthy mother would have bothered to do. She had secretly paid for a good school-ing and an undergraduate life at Cambridge where the girl worked extremely hard and became an exceptional mathematician. However scarce such types might be, the career open to feminine talent was slowly beginning to arrive. Lower down the scale of ability other chances were coming. A year after he had dramatized the Warrens' ways of life Shaw introduced into *Candida* Proserpine Garnett who works as secretary to the Socialist East End parson, Morell. 'Prossy' is 'a brisk little woman of about thirty, of the lower middle class', a capable registrar of Morell's speaking engagements and guardian of his movements who is well able to work a typewriter. It is unlikely that many vicars had secretaries then; if bishops had them, they were probably men. Secretaries were regarded as luxuries.

The headmaster of a large public school at the beginning of this century was not allowed one by his chairman of governors and had to write all his letters by hand. If he had suggested a young woman to help him, it would have been thought preposterous, and many senior business men at the time would have regarded women as undesirable intruders. In some commercial and legal firms with a conservative tradition hand-written letters were long the rule; duplicates for the files were taken by a male clerk from a copying press. But the feminine typists at last swarmed into the cities. This increased the range of mating; the middle-class girl did not have to wait at home for a husband or make the most of suburban dances and tennis-club acquaintances. That once exclusively masculine pre-serve, the City of London, has so much surrendered to the invasion that it has many shops providing for the clothing and adornment of women where once was only masculine haberdashery.

Thus something that Shaw wanted has come about: for him the necessary step in the liberation of women was the right to work where they wanted, to be trained for a variety of tasks, and to be admitted to the professions when their competence was proved. He would never admit that a person's right to own property was essential to his or her liberty. As a Socialist, and sometimes in economic matters writing as a non-Marxian Communist, he denounced all private ownership. But, if there were to be individual possessions, then women must have the same rights as men: among these the right to work in their chosen callings, as well as in the kitchen and the factory, was the most urgently needed. The ability to go out and earn has inevitably involved women in exhausting scrambles into overcrowded business areas. Getting in and out of central London at rush hours is no part of a sheltered life. Those who used to fight for a job now fight for a place on the 'bus or a strap-hanger's stance in the Tube. They do not give up in despair.

A monstrous injustice had been the right of the husband to control his wife's money. The property of wives was not legally their own until the passing of the Married Women's Property Act in 1882, which reduced, if it did not wholly abolish, a gross inequality. There was no legal barrier set up by the state to prevent the acquisition of economic freedom by taking jobs. But custom was powerful in the many self-governing professions which controlled their own rights of admission. The manly man still thought best of the womanly woman whose place was in the home. Whether frightened of competition in the office, the surgery, and the law-courts, or merely obstinate in his conception of home and duty, the manly man kept most of the gates shut until the end of the century. But custom was worn down and the door of *A Doll's House* was opened. The operative force was economic in the main and only doctrinal on the fringe. That Ibsen's play, seen and read by a tiny minority, had much to do with it was doubtful; but Shaw liked to believe that the dramatist with a cause to preach had a considerable pulpit. But it was not the obstinate, reactionary male who occupied the pews in his kind of church. Many who sat under him had already received the message.

During more than half of Shaw's life women had no political rights. John Stuart Mill had denounced this injustice in his book on *The Subjection of Women* published in 1869. But many Radicals and some Liberals were gradually being inclined to support female suffrage. Yet there had been no concession to women in the Reform Act of 1867. This increased, on a moderate scale and chiefly in towns, the size of the male electorate. In England there were still only two million voters and women had to wait another fifty years for enfranchisement. When the third Reform Act was passed in 1884 an amendment to extend the vote to women was supported by ninety-eight Conservatives as well as by a group of Liberals and Radicals, but Gladstone did not encourage support among members of his own party.

The Whig wing of the Liberal party contained strong opponents of the extended suffrage while the Conservatives were curiously divided. For example, in a vote in the House of Commons in 1897, the Ayes included the Conservative Balfour along with the Radicals Dilke and Haldane, while the Liberals Asquith and Bryce were among the Noes. The Socialists, with no parliamentary strength at that time, gave fairly solid support to the cause, but even among them there were a few anti-feminists. These could argue that women were too susceptible to specious pleading and might easily be coaxed for trifling reasons into voting for the wrong and reactionary candidate. That indeed had been to some extent the view of the Radical John Bright who at first championed and later opposed votes for women; his change of mind was caused by his belief that women were more likely to be seduced (politically) by Conservative clergymen of the Church of England. Had he lived to see the emotional seduction of young women achieved by film stars and 'pop singers' and the frenzied hysteria of mainly feminine crowds when such favourites appeared, he might have suffered further apprehension as to the poise and perspicacity of women electors.

So nothing was done though much was argued. In the early part of this century some of the most influential Liberal statesmen, whose party had swept into power in 1906 and was still in office in 1914, were obstinately opposed to admitting women to the roll of voters. They were confirmed in their antagonism to any change by the resort of the more indignant and even rabid suffragettes to arson and

Suffragettes advertising a meeting, 1914

physical violence. The moderates continued to plead their case ably and with abundant argument. The extremists, convinced that men were incapable of seeing reason and knowing that the Reform Act of 1832 had been won by threats of riot, became riotous and showed their endurance in prison by hunger strikes which led to the horrors of forcible feeding. But Ministers, refusing to accept the logic of the reasoning many, would not be stampeded by the law-breaking few.

The war of 1914–18 was a massacre of men. It was also a liberator of women. The nation, desperately in need of their labour and some of it of the heaviest and most exacting kind, could no longer deny the suffrage. Women swarmed out of the home into the factories and new branches of the forces. The pretence of a weaker sex became more nonsensical than ever. They had to be allowed the vote, but it was given grudgingly in the Act of 1918 and not on the same scale as the masculine enfranchisement. This was amended by another Act in 1928.

Shaw, since he was contemptuous of democracy, could not logi-
cally regard electoral reforms as vitally important. He did not sit on
the fence in discussing popular rights and capacities. He frankly stated
that increasing the number of voters only put more power into the
hands of the ignorant and stupid and this of course applied to both
sexes. The popular share in government, he thought, should be
restricted, not expanded. Accordingly he suggested examinations for
would-be voters, but how they were to be devised and carried out
he did not explain. In *Everybody's Political What's What* he said that
'for legislative purposes adult suffrage is out of the question' and that
'popular choice should be limited to those who have passed such
tests as we can devise of their wisdom, comprehension, knowledge,
and energy'. After that he strangely conceded the need 'for a popular
Parliament of men and women in equal numbers' which should be
allowed to criticize the government, pass votes of confidence or the
lack of it, and 'keep in touch with the people'.

No constitutional proposals could be more shadowy. A workable
examination, including tests of energy as well as knowledge, would
have to be medical as well as academic. Such probing of the millions
is an impossible idea. The life of the examiners, who would at once
be accused of party bias by the rejected citizens, would be unbearable.
And how could it be made certain that the 'popular Parliament'
would consist of men and women 'in equal numbers', since women
have been conspicuously unwilling to choose members of their own
sex. In the House of Commons elected in 1959 there were only
twenty-eight women, while women were in a slight majority on the
voting-lists.

Those who believe that economic power precedes political power
and in the right to work at a fair wage or to refuse work by striking
if the wage be deemed unfair, can hardly regard parliamentary democracy as a really important guarantor of freedom and justice. Since
Shaw's interest was in the economic status of women, extensions of
the suffrage were side issues for him.

Those whose ideal was still the womanly woman maintained that she should not be sullied by mingling with the coarse world of masculine politics. Surprisingly there were a number of women, capable in their own work and earning their own livings, who long continued to hold this view. The well-known novelist, Mrs Humphrey Ward, was one of the leaders of this party. But far the greater number of professional women were supporters of the suffrage movement and believed firmly that the achievement of the vote would not only remove an injustice to their sex, which Shaw could not deny, but greatly improve the membership and functioning of Parliament, on which point Shaw was sceptical.

As a Socialist he worked with women in committees and on platforms. He valued their energy and ability. He admired people who got things done instead of fussing over the election of others who would fail to get anything done. Democracy annoyed him because its electoral methods shuffled responsibility on to others, usually the glib and talkative people. If the woman, as he held, took the initiative in marriage-making, she could do no less for policy by taking the politician by the scruff of the neck and forcing him to abandon his evasive chatter and delays.

He was fascinated by 'boss types' of both sexes and was well aware that strong feminine personalities could be extremely influential and effective by going into action and sweeping men along. A great Victorian had exemplified that during his boyhood. Florence Nightingale, having by her own heroic labours done much to remedy the appalling inadequacy and administrative chaos of the Army's medical work during the Crimean War, set to work to reform hospital services at home. She put forward entirely new ideas about the planning of hospital buildings and the methods of hospital practice. The Nightingale Training School for Nurses, founded at St. Thomas's Hospital in 1860, marked the beginning of a new epoch in the tending of the sick. She then set out to expose the muddle and incompetent régime at the War Office itself where ingrained conservatism and departmental disputes made any action immensely difficult. She could do her work only by driving hesitant or reluctant

Florence Nightingale

men to take her counsels which became her commands. Her chief agent, Sidney Herbert, at the War Office, was on her side and was vigorously kept there. But his physical strength was unequal to his good will. Indefatigable herself, she helped to wear him out; and with his death Whitehall won and battles could go on being lost.

There were other fields in which her invincible determination could reveal social scandals and procure social improvements; her woman's eye scrutinized not only the hospitals but the work-houses and their infirmaries. Lytton Strachey pointed out that she had long anticipated the proposals of the Poor Law Commissioners Report which was issued in 1909, a year before her death at the age of ninety. She had never had a vote, but she had rarely taken no for an answer when she felt strongly enough about a course of conduct. She was a supreme politician who could never be in politics. As an unwomanly woman, she had made numerous enemies among the very manly men, but she died with her country's supreme award, the Order of Merit. Like Shaw's Millionairess she was a natural member of the 'boss class' and had confirmed his views that getting things done has little to do with democratic procedure.

Mrs Sidney Webb had served on the Poor Law Commission and her husband had supported her by drafting its Minority Report which contained Fabian Socialist views. Shaw had a profound admiration for Sidney Webb whose methodical, drab kind of Socialism and dedication to committee work were much disliked and gustily lampooned by H. G. Wells. Webb's genius was for industrious research, marshalling figures, and framing reformist proposals. To him Mrs Warren would have been a subject for inquiry and report, indexed as 'Bawds, remuneration of, and Brothels, high-class, conditions in'. But Vivie, with her aptitude for mathematics, would have been welcomed as his assistant statistician and might have made a first-class Fabian. Beatrice Webb shared Sidney's labours and his devoted way of life. Sidney became a Labour Member of Parliament and a Cabinet Minister, but he was not a great success away from his books and papers. Shaw would have said that this was another proof of the futility of Parliament. It wasted such abilities as Sidney Webb's. Fortunately, in his view, Beatrice was well away from the voters and the twaddling talkers whom they elected and so was able to go on with her research and formulations of policy based on that research.

Here was another unwomanly woman who spent most of her life without a vote and yet was effectively in the centre of politics. The Webbs made their home in Westminster where there were important people to be met and abundant strings to be pulled. They had no children, their home was a workshop, and their habits frugal. The Sunday suppers at their house in Grosvenor Road were gatherings of minds with thoughts above food. The hosts assembled elders worth capturing for their causes and young people, especially those with some leisure and money, whom they expected to be useful as docile committee members and potential volunteers in research. Cold mutton was combined with some warmth of argument and indoctrination. So the work was done, the committees reported, the pamphlets and the books were written, and the left wing of the Liberal party was instructed and slightly permeated with the gas-

Beatrice Webb   *Sidney Webb as Shaw first knew him*

and–water Socialism which the Fabians called 'collectivism' and the irreverent called 'Webb-footed bureaucracy'. Beatrice Webb worked away at the history of the workers as well as preparing their future. Her contacts with them were slight, but she could say 'It is the Cause, it is the Cause, my soul.' Like Florence Nightingale, the Lady of the Lamp, this Lady of the Blue Books had influence without office. The lives of both showed that a woman's place could be in the corridors of power where policies are made and pressures are exercised.

The matings of the Fabians and assorted philosophers with whom Shaw was associated during the first half of his life were sometimes a marriage of true minds; that applied to the Webbs and it was no less valid of his own union with Charlotte. Although he was a tranquilly and happily married man, he tended to generalize about the state of matrimony as though it were a continuous torment and to regard the ordinary English home as though it were a brick-box penitentiary. Consequently he was much more concerned with the right to escape from this supposed inferno than with the obligation to make the co-habitation of husbands and wives endurable if it could not be as enjoyable as the romantic hopes of the courting and the honeymoon had promised. He had to admit that rights and duties must go together in domesticity as in political society, but he put his emphasis on the former at the expense of the latter. If a married woman's place had to be in the home, this was not, he maintained, to be a life sentence.

She should know the way out of it and the same applied to the man. His right to escape was as fundamental as hers and this claim might be as necessary among the free thinkers and free lovers as among the most respectable attenders of church and chapel. Shaw's own affair with Mrs Besant, whose place had ceased to be in the parsonage proper to her married state, and his discovery of her idea of a free contractual relationship had taught him to be vigilant and ready to run for his life. So in his exposition of sexual unions suitable to a civilized community he was insistent on easy release. There must be a ladder at the bedroom window for the sudden departure of the disillusioned and back-doors must be kept unlocked. This was not to make adultery easy but to make long years of mutual exasperation impossible.

The Preface to his play *Getting Married,* written twelve years after the author's own visit to the Registrar, provides a conducted tour round the hell which Shaw himself had missed but regarded as normal in the villadom of every suburban street. In this long and always lively essay he usefully reminded the British reader that marriage is an institution with such remarkable varieties of principle and practice that the name means nothing without further definition. It includes in our own United Kingdom English sacramental and civil marriage, both terminable by divorce, Roman Catholic indis-soluble marriage, Scottish marriage, Irish marriage, re-marriage of divorced persons, and marriage with a first cousin which some hold to be incestuous. Elsewhere, ranging from Turkey to South Dakota, Shaw descried still more varieties of union recognized and deemed respectable in their own states. Polygamy is lawful within the British Commonwealth in some large parts of which the woman's place is by law and custom the harem and not the home. 'In Sweden,' he added, 'one of the most civilized countries in the world, a marriage is dissolved if both parties wish it, without any question of conduct.' With his conviction that the essence of a satisfactory marriage bond must be its fragility in case of need Shaw discovered Stockholm to be the most sensible of capitals. No Doll's Houses, no imprisonments there.

In *The Revolutionist's Handbook* it is forecast by John Tanner that neither in England nor in America would a straight proposal to make an end of marriage be acceptable: yet 'nothing is more certain that in both countries the progressive modification of the marriage contract will be continued until it is no more onerous or irrevocable than any ordinary commercial deed of partnership'. The right to quit must be established without question. So far, so free. But what of the Life Force with which the Revolutionist was so well acquainted? Tanner had to admit its results, adding that 'the essential function of marriage is the continuance of the human race'. The wedded might part at will. But the children had to remain somewhere. The problems of the home involve duties of parental care as well as rights of parental escape. It was not a matter to which Shaw gave enough thought. The urgent point for him was the easy termination 'of all unhappy, improper, and uncomfortable marriages'. He went the whole way in advocating unconditional divorce in the Preface to *Getting Married*. His concluding summary begins:

'(1) Make divorce as easy, as cheap, and as private as a marriage.

(2) Grant divorce at the request of either party, whether the other consents or not; and admit no other ground than the request, which should be made without stating any reasons.'

Here is a Bill of Rights indeed—for the adults. But what of the juniors? Shaw had no children and was apt to dismiss too lightly the difficulties of family life. In this Preface he answered the obvious question about the children of a broken home by saying, 'I must not flippantly reply make them all Wards in Chancery: yet that would be enough to put any sensible person on the track of the reply.' The further advice and explanation are sketchy and impractical. Nobody would deny that a home with parental quarrels simmering and with brawls and abusive outbursts always possible is a deplorable place for any child. But is it less awful than being removed to a detested boarding-school or deposited with foster-parents approved (and sometimes carelessly and disastrously approved) by a local authority? The Town Hall officials may do their best, but the problem of settling the children of hopelessly incompatible couples or of criminal types has its complications and subtleties beyond the capacity of a civil servant who has to follow precedents and instructions and dares not risk dismissal by having ideas of his own.

The bureaucrat as distributor and guardian of the parentless children whose number will be greatly increased by making divorce as cheap and easy as possible! It is a thought so dismal that one can hardly bear to think in detail of all the difficulties involved. At this point the subject becomes too big for discussion in anything less than a Counter-Preface of the same length. *Getting Unmarried or the Ever-Open Exit Examined* might be the title.

CHAPTER SEVEN

Bill of Health

IF a man survives to be ninety-four, it is apparent that he has lived sensibly in order to live long. To be abstemious was easy for Shaw. He became a vegetarian at twenty-five. This decision he attributed partly to a large appetite for the poetry and exemplary opinions of Shelley and partly to a periodic recurrence of severe headaches which he attributed to the eating of meat. This trouble may have been mitigated but did not disappear when he altered his diet. Since abstention from meat was increasing, there were more vegetarian restaurants available and their prices were of a kind that he could meet. He wasted nothing on tobacco and did not endanger his throat and lungs with that solace. To him smoking was a filthy habit which created a filthy smell, especially where there was heavy use of pipes and cigars and small use of ventilation, as in some Bohemian company as well as frowsty railway-carriages.

His natural vitality was enormous; stimulants were unnecessary and unwanted. Mrs Patrick Campbell said that if he were given a beef-steak no woman in London would be safe in his company. In the years of his 'affairs' it was perhaps well that he could not afford to buy champagne and that the sparkle of the evening had to be conversational only. According to Hesketh Pearson, Shaw did serve wine when he was entertaining later in life; he said that he chose it himself after a personal sampling. His asceticism did not include the notion that alcohol was a poison fermented by the devil and pro-hibition essential to the safety of society. So he did not campaign against the narcotics that he avoided. But his young experience of life with a tippling father naturally inclined him to be a teetotaller.

The meatless regimen had to be abandoned for a while late in his life. When he was eighty-one he was in danger of dying from pernicious anæmia and he was cured by doses of liver extract; to him it was an act of treason to take this carnal nourishment, but his wife was adamant. Apart from that his diet, including eggs, which are meat in the making, sufficed for close on seventy years and gave him the long-continued health and superlative energy whose occasional interruptions were, he believed, caused by overwork. They were remedied, with Charlotte firmly insisting, by removal from home for short holidays in Britain and longer ones abroad or at sea.

The diet was deliberately aimed at physical and mental efficiency; seeking enjoyment was never a part of his intentions. Self-indulgence he despised. Happiness, he knew, was a by-product of unfrustrated and satisfying activity and not an end to be pursued for itself. 'I flatly declare,' he said, 'that a man fed on whisky and dead bodies cannot do the finest work of which he is capable.' There may be something in that, but he was thinking primarily of brain-work and sessions at the desk and not of fitness for exacting physical labour.

There is one mystery in his chart of health. At the end of May, 1881, when he was twenty-four and working hard and vainly at his early novel-writing, he is said to have been seized with smallpox. It was a subject on which, though not usually secretive, he kept remarkably silent and one may wonder whether he really was afflicted with so grave a disease. He was living with his mother and possibly one of his sisters in Fitzroy Street; according to St John Ervine's account 'he was confined to his room for three weeks'. In an untidy, ill-run house the chance of the infection spreading was obvious. But his mother and sister apparently suffered no harm. He was not sent to hospital and he was not long isolated. To us, with our apprehensions about epidemics, the treatment seems strangely casual. His recovery was rapid. In June he went to stay with his uncle, Dr Walter Gurley, who was practising at Leyton and would obviously not have received him if there had been any fear of contagion. It has been said that Shaw grew a beard to hide the pock-marks, but beards are grown for more reasons than concealment. Is it possible that he was not a victim of smallpox as generally understood, but of some minor ailment causing eruptions on the skin?

The visit to Leyton introduced him to a kind of medical practice which he was to describe later in the Preface to *The Doctor's Dilemma* (1906) and to exemplify in the text of the play. Here was the world of bitter Victorian poverty, of the patient who could not afford to pay a doctor more than a pittance and of the doctor who, with no state medical service to maintain him, could not afford to pay for a good suit or to be punctual in meeting his bills at the food-shops. When Dr Gurley went to Leyton it was a pleasant, country-house kind of district on the edge of Epping Forest. Then the overspill of East London covered its fields with brick-boxes whose main population was made up of 'clerks supporting families on fifteen shillings a week'. Those able to pay reasonable fees for medical attention drifted away from the depressed suburb that Leyton had become. It was foolish of Uncle Walter to remain as he did. Left with those who could scarcely find sixpence for a consultation, he was ruined.

One of this kind appears in the play as the wretched Dr Blenkinsop, shabby and humiliated by his poverty in the presence of his one-time fellow students who are now Harley Street big-wigs. He explains that his patients are clerks and shop-workers who cannot afford to be ill. When they break down, it is impossible to order them expensive foods and holidays abroad. He is miserably conscious of his own inability to provide the correct treatments in these economic conditions. Furthermore, he can neither feed nor clothe himself properly on the product of such a practice. He is racked with indigestion and is becoming consumptive.

This is, no doubt, an extreme picture. But during most of Shaw's lifetime a young doctor, instead of immediately finding full employment in a decently remunerated Health Service, was expected to buy himself into a practice. This meant the possession of private means or procuring a loan at a high rate of interest because the security was so slight. If he had no capital and would not or could not borrow, he had to look for a suitable district, house himself as respectably as he could, put a brass plate on his door, and wait for callers. In 1882 young Dr Conan Doyle from Edinburgh came south to do that in Southsea. He had to stand at the window and watch people as they looked at his name (at the rate of one a minute sometimes) and then moved away. But he was a good mixer and a good games player, qualities one does not suspect in Blenkinsop. Also he could write stories and later, with difficulty and delay, sell them. If he had been able to buy himself into a busy practice and had been fully occupied and reasonably paid from the start, the public might never have had Sherlock Holmes, that triumphant child of a doctor's poverty.

Shaw denounced as 'a murderous absurdity' the commercial and competitive doctoring which lasted almost to the end of his life. At the top was Harley Street with its big names and big incomes. At a rather lower social level the profession included the fairly prosperous servants of the middle-class need, such as Dr Gurley had once been, and the wretchedly paid attenders on the then wretchedly paid working-class, as Dr Gurley became and as Blenkinsop is presented in *The Doctor's Dilemma*. A curious light is thrown on the vicissitudes of economic life by the overcrowding of the medical profession at the end of last century when its lower ranks were wretchedly rewarded, and by the shortage of doctors in the nineteen-sixties when they could be certain of their jobs and incomes. Shaw in 1905 spoke of thousands too many. At the Trades Union Congress in 1964 a delegate of the Medical Practitioners Union spoke of thousands too few, with the inadequate number constantly reduced by emigration.

Entry to the profession is no longer limited by the need to buy a share in a practice, but the soaring price of houses and surgery space began to require an investment in property which the average young doctor could not face. When Conan Doyle went, quite unknown, to Southsea he was able to find a house of reasonable quality in a good enough street and this he could rent for forty pounds a year with no compulsion to pay a penny in advance. Shaw campaigned for a public medical service and got it when Aneurin Bevan's National

Health Act was implemented in July, 1948. Now there need be no
more brass-plated Doyles looking vainly out of the window. There
need be no more Blenkinsop incomes. But the so-called Age of
Affluence, which was then beginning, did not solve all the doctors'
dilemmas or provide the compulsorily contributing patients with all
they could expect. With the 'N.H.' providing abundant opportunities
for work at home the newly qualified were often eager to avoid
working in bleak industrial areas or to escape altogether from the
socialized medicine of the new Britain by going abroad.

Shaw's criticism of the old medical methods, while it exaggerated
some faults, had a core of logic. It does seem absurd that doctors
should depend for their living on the continuance of illness in the
community. So the picture could be drawn of the wretched medicos'
ruin if they did the job so efficiently as greatly to reduce, if they could
not wholly abolish, the various maladies and epidemics on which
they could be unkindly described as battening. It was part of Shaw's
complaint that doctors whose incomes were on the Blenkinsop level
welcomed compulsory vaccination because it brought them a flow

THE DOCTOR'S DILEMMA, *Royal Court, 1906*

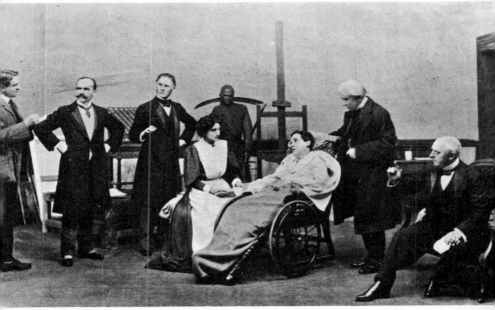

of half-crowns for the mass inoculations which he regarded as dangerous and unnecessary. The practitioners of the Harley Street grade, or at least some of them, were accused of suggesting unnecessary operations and inventing new ones to provide profitable work.

In *The Doctor's Dilemma,* the character of Sir Cutler Walpole is introduced as one of the prosperous wielders of the knife. He has discovered a small and useless attachment of the human interior called the nuciform sac. This, the patient can be told, is a potential cause of toxic conditions. It may be harmless, but it may be a menace. People are safer without it. So why not get rid of it? The sac could be removed without danger or disadvantage to the ordinary person and with great personal advantage to Sir Cutler. The surgeon, said Shaw, is always on safe ground. If it is alleged that an operation was needless and useless, he can always reply that, though nothing terrible was discovered when the examination was made, something dreadful might have occurred if nothing had been done.

There was a historical background to the ridicule of Sir Cutler and his nuciform sac. King Edward the Seventh had been extremely ill with gastric pains before his Coronation; this distress was diagnosed as inflammation of the vermiform appendix, which is not usually described with the adjective meaning worm-shaped. The royal appendix was successfully removed with the publicity which so august an occasion made inevitable. This species of sac and its operative treatment were in the news and soon in the vogue. 'There is a fashion,' said Shaw, 'in operations as there is in sleeves and skirts.' He added, 'There are men and women whom the operating table seems to fascinate, half-alive people who, through vanity or hypochondria or a craving to be constant objects of anxious attention, lose such feeble sense as they ever had of the value of their own organs or limbs.'

Whether or not that is generally true, Mayfair, with the money to pay high fees, became a profitable market for those advising and executing the up-to-date excisions which had been made fashionable by the royal example. A wealthy person who is to undergo an operation, however slight, will naturally want to have a star performer for the job. Competition for the services of the surgeons most spoken of resulted in some charges which seem colossal considering the value of money in the Edwardian years. If there was nothing to be made by removing portions of poor people in hospitals, the experience was useful, as Shaw reminded his readers, for Sir Cutler and his kind. Such practice could add precision, if it did not guarantee perfection, to their handicraft when it was employed on the good payer lodged in a costly nursing home in which the surgeons themselves might have a useful financial interest.

And so it went on. There were fads and cults in the higher medical circles. Not all were as expensive for the patient as the major surgery, but they offered profitable opportunities. In the nineteen-twenties there were the Cutler Walpoles who could not hear of a tonsil without demanding to eradicate such deplorable cover for invading germs. There was also a joint offensive on the gums carried out by doctors and dentists together. Here again poison was supposed to be nestling. The word 'pyorrhæa' was much employed in diagnoses and aches and pains of all kinds were attributed to this oral infection: the remedy was copious extraction of teeth. After that gastric troubles were to be healed by calling in the practitioners of colonic irrigation. Next treatments with various kinds of ray were regarded as pouring new life into the sickly until it was suggested that rays of unknown potency might do as much for destruction of tissue as for stimulation of vitality. Then came the hunt for allergies and patients were copiously pricked to discover their reactions. What Shaw had written about medical fashions twenty years earlier remained true of the profession whose patients continued to think of its members as infallible paragons of scientific wisdom.

After that came psychoanalysis. It presented some very old truths about 'the rooted troubles of the brain', familiar to the author of *Macbeth,* with a new range of investigation and a portentously formidable vocabulary. Its practitioners, suave, consoling, and astute, were always ready with an impressive classical term to describe a common distress. The conventional doctors had long been playing that game with their use of Latin in prescriptions. The psychoanalysts played it in polysyllabic Greek as well. If it consoled anxious folk frightened by crowds to say that they were afflicted with agarophobia, why not gratify them with abundance of this palaver? Since *soma* is the Greek for body they used the term 'psychosomatic' when advising a patient that his physical pains were caused by mental or emotional distress and that the new therapy could rid him of his aches along with his anxieties. Shaw could not accuse the priests of the new cult with more misdoing than exploiting public gullibility and pandering to the vanity of those who would pay lavishly for a tactful and sympathetic listener to their flood of self-pity and often imaginary grievances. They were not making money with new forms of Walpole's cutlery and they did not demand the use of vaccines to which he was violently and constantly opposed. That at least was an advance in Shaw's valuation of the profession he attacked.

As the years went by he could watch some of the medical procedure which he had ridiculed pass out of fashion and disappear. He could see a variety of cures abandoned as useless or even exposed as doing more harm than good. So after a while tonsils and teeth were not condemned to general eradication without trial and were shown some mercy if they could prove their inoffensiveness. It was increasingly realized that tonsils were filters as well as germ traps. The rays of the supposedly magic lanterns were less lavishly applied. That medical faiths should be exposed as superstitions was gratifying to Shaw. He could expect to see psychotherapy also losing its status: since his death it has been maintained in more advanced circles that emotional disturbances and unbalanced personalities will be much better treated in future by physical treatment. The hormone has the limelight now.

Shaw's attack on privately paid doctoring and on the fashionable surgeons who were mingling excessive extortion, as he thought, with needless excision was to some extent justified. The specialist who now attends a hospital draws a regular and considerable Health Service salary and so has no temptation to add to his surgical work because he has a large family or an extravagant wife. In demanding a public health service Shaw was saving the rich doctor from avarice as well as the poor from degradation. At the same time he paid fair tribute to the genuine devotion to work in the case of most of the profession; he fully acknowledged their endurance of long hours, sudden and perhaps unnecessary calls, and interrupted nights. He was aware too of the time wasted by the exasperating stupidity and egotism of some patients. If the conduct of medicine on pay-as-you-go, commercial lines was an absurdity, possibly murderous, the nation, he said, was to blame for putting its doctors in the position of tradesmen who dared not offend the customer and had to deliver their goods and services to suit the public taste.

In apportioning the responsibility for this, Shaw censured the wealthy seekers of fashionable cures as fools and faddists who would swallow any novelty if it had the approval of the medical mandarins and was marketed with a fine-sounding name. The poor, in his opinion, were no better. They put up with the causes of their diseases, such as abominable housing in insanitary urban conditions, because, he said, they were too silly to be Socialists and believed that the essential national and municipal reforms would only bring higher taxation and additions to their rates. What they wanted in Mean Street was the doctor as a conjuror offering magical potions at popular prices; he must always be ready with something in a bottle to which he had attached a Latin label. In other words they looked for safety supplied at cut prices and with no need to live carefully and amend their habits.

Shaw often spoilt a case by overstressing the follies that infuriated him. The Preface to *The Doctor's Dilemma* must be read with that in mind. It must also be remembered that he came out on the winning side. He had asked for 'a body of men trained and paid by the country to keep the country in health' and he lived to see his policy prevail. 'Nothing,' he had said, 'is more dangerous than a poor doctor.' The Health Service medico, while he has his grievances and does not hesitate to grumble, is not an anxious solicitor for customers and has an income which would have left poor Blenkinsop faint with astonishment.

Shaw's idea that too healthy a community could be the ruin of practitioners living on their fees and so gave them a vested interest in illness was plainly an exaggeration. A public health service does not and cannot produce public health to the extent of leaving surgeries unvisited and hospitals unwanted. Pregnancies, more numerous than ever, have to be watched and babies born. Accidents abound and the world in which Everyman is or soon will be his own motorist (and often a reckless one) produces hospital cases at a rate of a quarter of a million a year apart from its stimulation of the funeral trade.

The longer people live the more physical failings they may have to endure. That the expectation of life has greatly increased is the doctors' victory. (Shaw would have denied this, attributing the added years to more sensible and hygienic ways of living.) At the same time old age must add to the doctors' work. Consequently there is now a department of medicine called 'gerontology', which translated from the Greek means the science of coping with senility. Bodies do not continue without strain and stress, loss of mobility, and what Sir Winston Churchill so well called 'the surly advance of decrepitude'. The memory fails too, quite apart from weakening of the mind. Some degree of arthritis is natural to advancing years. The old are prone to accidents on slippery floors and in frozen streets, both of which are bad places on which to collapse. Severe damage is easily done. Shaw himself fell in the last year of his life while pruning trees in his garden. He broke a leg and had to be taken to hospital, where he was fretful in confinement. Then kidney trouble set in and the end came. Had he been less obstinately active he might have reached his century; this would have befitted one who had commended Methuselism as humanity's way to greater wisdom. He had to learn that if doctors make the span of life more elastic they cannot do the same for limbs and are very far from putting themselves out of work.

There have been remarkable advances in the discovery of therapeutic drugs and new treatments since he wrote *The Doctor's Dilemma* and he lived to see diabetes deprived of its worst effects by insulin. The vaccines, which he denounced as unnatural and even murderous, have justified their use. A wide range of inoculations has proved effective without involving serious risk in many cases. Smallpox is very rare in Britain and typhoid, despite occasional outbreaks, is quickly isolated and, when it does occur in epidemic form as it did in Aberdeen in 1964, it does not kill as it once did. Armies no longer lose more men by disease than they do in battle, as happened during the Boer War. Diphtheria, which used to out-Herod Herod in its slaughter of the young innocent, has been almost totally removed from the list of fatal scourges by immunization.

The chief peril of the old, pneumonia, has been deprived of its terrors. Tuberculosis has been triumphantly diminished. Penicillin is only one of the more recent discoveries that has powerfully contributed to longer survival. Improved anaesthetics have given the surgeons more time to do their work and their patients a much easier passage from the operating table to their beds of recovery. None the less, because of and not despite the new preservatives of life, we must have our gerontologists busily at work. Hospitals are always full; more, bigger, and better hospitals are in demand. The doctors, instead of joining the unemployed, complain of overwork, excessively large panels, and crowded clinics and consulting rooms.

There have also been failures and disasters. Cancer still defeats research, including the vivisection which Shaw detested and denounced. Loathing cruelty of all kinds, whether it was occasioned by the sportsman or the carnivore, he spoke as well as wrote against it. Once he was horrified to find himself on an anti-vivisection platform surrounded by wealthy women wearing the furs of trapped animals and the plumage of slaughtered birds. He could not share a humanitarian spirit so limited in its scope. The amount of benefit which vivisection has brought to the human invalid is a matter of bitter contention. One thing cannot be disputed. The campaign against it has not prevailed. The Home Office Report issued in 1964 told of nearly two hundred and seventy thousand experiments made by close on six thousand licensees of which more than seventy thousand were performed without anaesthesia. The Home Office inspectors were fully occupied, making two thousand visits. They reported that the animals used were 'satisfactorily accommodated'. To house the victims properly seems a small mercy. Shaw's comment on such a finding might have burned the paper on which he wrote.

His tirades against the unscientific scientist have been justified by the necessity to abandon certain treatments because unforeseen results have proved either unavailing or even disastrous. That experiments must sometimes fail is obvious, but to put them into practice without awareness of their monstrous perils is a crime beyond forgiveness. The misshapen and crippled babies produced by the administration of thalidomide to pregnant women has been the most horrible of these blunders and has tragically excused Shaw's indictment of reckless over-confidence in the output of the chemical laboratories. He ridiculed the superstitions of science as more absurd than those of the most primitive faiths and would have been appalled by the way in which politicians, now demanding more and more science in the schools and universities, have used the word as a magical incantation for realizing the old dream of an elixir of life. He was far too sweeping, but we cannot forget thalidomide.

There is no need in Shaw's philosophy of old age for gerontology to come to the rescue. In his vision of triumphant Methuselism, the Ancients and She-Ancients, living to be at least seven hundred, have become the fountains of all wisdom. He worked on *Back to Methuselah*, which he called his Metabiological Pentateuch, when he was in his sixties. It was published in 1921 when he was sixty-five and presented in London by Sir Barry Jackson at the Court Theatre three years later. Since its theme is the superiority of the long-livers over the short-livers, it is curious to find him ending the Preface to his Pentateuch, which runs to eighty pages of his prose at its most vigorous, with the statement, 'My sands are running out. The exuberance of 1901 has aged into the garrulity of 1920 . . . I am doing the best I can at my age. My powers are waning; but so much the better for those who found me unbearably brilliant when I was in my prime.' He hoped that younger hands engaged on this theme would leave him far behind.

This announcement of a dwindling force is nonsense. His prime was a long one. He had just finished *Heartbreak House* and *Saint Joan* was still to come, acclaimed as his best play by many and now a modern classic on the stage. According to his Methuselist doctrine he should not have spoken of dwindling powers but proclaimed, 'With my years I go from strength to strength. My experience is ever riper and my thinking ever deeper. The best is still to come. Wait and see me at a hundred.' It is true that garrulity did set in after 1930 and that the plays of his last two decades are too discursive to be dramatic. It is true also that there is a flood of somewhat random talk in the three middle pieces of his Pentateuch, but the first of the five, set in the Garden of Eden, and the last, post-dated to 31,920 A.D., are theatrically effective. Those who saw them on the stage will not have forgotten the experience though they may have yawned a little through the central reaches. The start and finish contain some of the most striking passages that he ever wrote for the players, led in 1924 by Edith Evans and Cedric Hardwicke.

The subject is the conquest of senile decay by the working of creative evolution in which the human will is the creative and victorious force. Man, according to Shaw, could decide his own future, even to a miraculous extent, instead of allowing himself to be developed fortuitously or destroyed foolishly by submission to the Darwinian theory of natural selection. In the Preface he said, 'Men do not live long enough. They are mere children when they die.' 'If,' he continued, 'man now fixes his term of life at three score and ten years he can equally fix it at three hundred or three thousand . . . This is not fantastic speculation: it is deductive biology.'

By this he meant that many species of animal life had achieved

MR. BERNARD SHAW'S "METABIOLOGICAL PENTATEUCH": ADAM (MR. COLIN KEITH-JOHNSTON), EVE (MISS GWEN FFRANGÇON-DAVIES) AND THE SERPENT (MISS EDITH EVANS, WITHIN THE HOOD) IN PART I, "IN THE BEGINNING."

successful variations through creative evolution. They had changed and advanced by their own determination and not by the luck of chance survival. What they had done man could do, overcoming his wasting and murderous maladies by prudence instead of pills and by resolving with all his will to live on and on and learn more and more. In legend, or for any who still believe that every word of the Bible was divinely inspired and remains completely true, longevity had happened before. Why not again? Let man discard the nonsense of the determinist believers in selection without choice and the non-sense of the doctors whose cures are at best alleviations and do not cure. Thus man could make senility a form of prolonged juvenility in the flesh and the source of increasing sagacity in the mind. Having set his body and brain in order he could put his house in order too and produce a world for the wisely adult and the sanely civilized to live in.

Back to Methuselah was to be Shaw's beginning of a Bible for creative evolution. Some crudity he modestly confessed, but it would carry on the tradition of religious legend and mingle teaching with story-telling in the manner of the medieval miracle plays. There has been a constant human dream that people as well as things were bigger and better in the past. The Romans looked back to a reign of Saturn, peaceful and golden days. The Hebrews had a vision of primeval giants in the land and of men so healthy that they could defy old age. Methuselah's father Enoch lived, says the Book of Genesis, until he was three hundred and sixty-five. During that time he 'walked with God' but what share of divine excellence he thus attained was not apparently passed on for the instruction of his fellows. It must have been inconsiderable since Jehovah had to destroy them for their sins, sparing only Noah with his family and the animals.

Methuselah himself lived to be nine hundred and sixty-nine, to what advantage we are not told. Evidently he did not need doctors. At the age of one hundred and eighty-seven he begat Lamech and his son lived to be seven hundred and seventy-seven, having fathered Noah who reached five hundred years at least. That Noah 'planted a vineyard' and was sometimes over-fond of its products may explain his failure to surpass the great Methuselist example. Shaw, with his loathing of self-indulgence in food and drink, could have seen the affair so.

His Methuselists, who appear in the last phase of his Pentateuch, are going strong at eight hundred. His Ancients and their predecessors have willed their way to the defeat of disease: death may come to them by accident. They may, as happened to their author, have a fatal fall. These vessels of the Life Force are well preserved because they have overcome the pleasures of the senses and are 'incarnate mind'. The day is ahead 'when there will be no people only thought'. The Superman will not be man at all. After passing a million goals men and women will pass on by redemption from the flesh 'to the vortex freed from matter, to the whirlpool in pure intelligence that, when the world began, was a whirlpool in pure force'. It is not a future which will appeal to the average sensual reader or playgoer. But Shaw foresaw in 1920 the ultimate destruction of mankind by his own lunacy, a possibility which the scientists of nuclear fission were soon to emphasize. But nothing to him was inevitable. His creative evolution is a doctrine of free choice. Man can be wise if he will and must not permit himself to die before he is out of his intellectual childhood.

One may wonder if Shaw would have written his Pentateuch twenty years later in his life. Had he proved that the fuller the experience, the better the deed? His latest plays were too rambling to attract and hold large audiences and his final excursions into politics do not reveal an accumulated and intensified sagacity. His contemptuous rejection of democracy made him sympathetic to the dictators who became insanely bellicose and ruled by savage persecution of all opinions but those of themselves and their applauding partisans.

To this he would presumably have replied that, as he had to exist in a world of short-livers, he was bound by the condition of others in his time. The progress to longevity would have to be gradual. Creative evolution, even with will-power functioning to the full, cannot evolve at a gallop. It could not possibly carry one twentieth-century individual to the kind of sage maturity which he had imagined for mankind in his vision of epochs rather than of years. He had not postulated speed. The year 31,920 A.D., he could have pointed out, is not exactly around the corner. As one of the short-lived breed he had done his best.

For him the body had to be kept in health because it is the container of the brain. In so far as he conceived of rapture it could only be gained in his view of happiness by intellectual activity. The pleasure which accompanies the perfect working of the limbs and senses he regarded as the indulgence of careless livers for the day. There might be crowded hours of glorious life but they could only be discovered in the head. In 1922, while arguing with Clive Bell the art-critic, whom he playfully called a 'fat-head and voluptuary' for enjoying wine, women, song, and cheroots, Shaw stated his delight in pure thought. 'Intellect is a passion; and its activity and satisfaction, which can be maintained from seven years old to a hundred and seven, if you can manage to live so long, are keenly pleasurable if the brain is strong enough for the exercise. Descartes must have got far more pleasure out of life than Casanova.' (Descartes had declared, 'I think; therefore I am.') In *Back to Methuselah,* one of the characters says, 'The body always ends by being a bore. Nothing remains beautiful and interesting except thought, because the thought is life.' To this the Ancients reply with a complete agreement.

The irony of Shaw's Methuselism lies in the fact that during his time man was beginning to live longer but showed no sign of becoming politically wiser. Cleverness multiplied; statesmanship did not. The inventors raced on with their astounding discoveries. The space travellers could go on orbit in the stratosphere. The first men on the moon will no doubt make their landing within twenty years of Shaw's death and then live to return. But all the technological achievements have not added to the sum of peace, tolerance, and sensible co-existence on earth. Disarmament conferences have been a routine that does not disarm. The weapons accumulate with growing capacity for the destruction of millions.

There is no belief that the old growing older gain greater capacity to govern and that the young should profit from the wisdom gathered by their grandfathers. Such a belief, if it existed, would be hard to justify. The seniors, be they shrewd or silly, must now expect to be elbowed out of office at ever earlier stages. Insistently the younger generation is knocking at the door, but it is not a classroom door to be entered by students of politics and economics eager for enlightenment and hungry for the ripe fruits of elderly experience. The doors which they force open lead to the corridors of power. Understandably it is position not preaching which lures them forward. It is no world for Methuselists. Such ancients as we have can end their prolonged existence by sitting on seaside promenades and wondering whether their pensions will see them through.

Meanwhile they have continually an added year or two in which to watch the tide move in and out. The elders who are sent into retirement at sixty are much younger in strength and spirit than their grandparents would have been at that age. To that kind of very limited Methuselism they have been brought partly by more careful habits: two major wars with their strict rationing have taught the people of many nations that it is possible to thrive on far less than was eaten sixty years ago by all who could afford it. One has only to look at the many and monstrous courses of an Edwardian banquet or the hotel menus of the time to be astonished at the amount provided and mostly consumed. But abstention from overeating is not the only explanation. It is Shaw's despised doctors who have in so many cases raised the Biblical span of seventy years to eighty or more. Their life-extending techniques and innovations have in the main turned longevity from a fortunate curiosity into a normal expectation.

At least so it seems when the statistics are compiled and the causes computed. Shaw would have scorned the idea and delivered a homily on our misuse of the evidence. He continued to keep in print the Preface to *The Doctor's Dilemma* in which he had written off modern medicine as a pretentious and pestilent fraud. The comedy of the play continues to delight. Here is the Attic salt of Shavian wit showered richly over the characters and the dialogue. But the message must now be taken with the other kind of salt, not in grains but in handfuls. Harley Street is still there. Of its more august figures it can be said by the cynic that they are chiefly brilliant in persuading relatives that the patient died in the best possible hands. But in fact they are managing much better than that. For Shaw, as a Socialist, consolation came in the National Health Service, but if he could see all that is happening he would not relish the revelations about the amount and price of the medicines and drugs which he denounced being ordered by the new-model and prospering Blenkinsops at public expense. Since in his later years he was as angry with the tax-gatherers as he had been with the doctors he has escaped by death some further exasperation and we have missed the entertainment of the scathing prose which the new high cost of curing would have evoked.

CHAPTER EIGHT

Politics and Platforms

W HEN Shaw was a young man in Dublin he took the nationalist and anti-English line; on reaching England he soon found plenty of rude things to say about that country and all its ways and he continued to say them throughout his life. But he found it a good enough place in which to remain. He stayed in and around London for more than seventy years unmolested except by his intemperate and pestering admirers. If he ever felt, as Hamlet did of Denmark, that Britain was a prison, he was at liberty to leave his cell.

His return visits to Ireland were very few; he did not retire, as other writers of the rebellious kind have done, to seek a European refuge. He carped but he did not quit. His refusal to go made at least a partial answer to his incessant criticism of British rule. He did indeed have at one time a good cause for complaint in the follies of the Stage Censorship which banned one of his long plays and two of his short ones until common sense broke into the Lord Chamberlain's office. The vetoes deprived him of theatre royalties which in these cases would not have been large and were inconsiderable when the bans were lifted. He could always freely print what the actors were not allowed to speak and a thousand people must have read *Mrs Warren's Profession* for every one who wanted to see it on the stage when it was liberated. No article of his, however revolutionary in its suggestions, brought him into the dock of a police court. While early contemptuous of democracy because it dithered, and ultimately sympathetic to dictatorships because they got things done, he must have known that his writings would have brought him continual persecution and suppression in a police state. That he was well aware of this is shown by his staying where he was when he had plenty of money and could, as an author with no ties, live where he chose and in the end much more cheaply owing to the crushing impact of British taxation after two world wars. But the villa in Switzerland, which became so attractive to retired film stars and practising writers in the best-seller class, never appealed to him. He could go on railing without stint or interference in the land of his choice and his denunciation.

His political interests were keenly aroused when he was twenty-six. In September, 1882, he happened to hear the powerful orator, Henry George, expounding his panacea for social injustice, the single tax based on land values. When this policy was favourably occupying Shaw's mind he was told by a leading Socialist, H. M. Hyndman, that the single tax would get nowhere, that Comprehensive Socialism was the only hope, and that he should go away and read Karl Marx. This he obediently did, applying himself to *Das Kapital* at the British Museum reading-room. He was vastly impressed for a while by the Marxian thesis, but later rejected the economic theory of value which was its basis; but he retained his admiration for Marx as a Jeremiah prophetically announcing the doom of capitalism while castigating its crimes.

The term revolutionary can have what meanings the champions and opponents of social upheaval like to give it. Shaw used the word of himself but he never supported the overthrow of capitalism by physical violence. Hesketh Pearson has recounted a stormy episode in which Shaw as agitator was on the fringe of serious trouble. In November, 1887, he took part in a great march to Trafalgar Square organized in order to assert the right of free speech against police prohibitions of such parades. Their veto had been made possible by an Act which gave them the right to 'regulate' processions. He was a member of a contingent which assembled at Clerkenwell Green and, being already in high repute as a soap-box orator, he delivered a speech. In it he counselled orderly conduct. On their way west it was found that another section of the marchers ahead of them was being driven back by the police using their truncheons. By scattering

Henry George   G. K. Chesterton

its numbers the Clerkenwell party, or most of it, with Shaw included, reached Trafalgar Square where cavalry had been called out to support the police when violence broke out. Shaw suffered no worse than jostling.

A handsome Scottish laird, R. B. Cunninghame Graham, who had become a Socialist of the romantic, freedom-loving type, as it were a Cavalier among Roundheads, was arrested and sent to prison for six weeks. Since he had been hurt in the affray he had the good fortune to spend his time in the infirmary and not in the cells. Another sent to prison for his part in what came to be known as Bloody Sunday was John Burns, then a redoubtable preacher of Socialism but later Liberal M.P. for Battersea and a member of the Liberal and far from Socialistic government from 1906 to 1914. Shaw came out of the affair undamaged and also unimpressed by the results of such uneven conflict. He saw no advantage to be gained by inviting the defeat that was inevitable when the unarmed and unorganized demonstrators were confronted by armed and organized forces.

When it was planned to arrange another march to the Square,

Mrs Besant, who had joined the previous procession, vigorously demanded that there should be no surrender to the authorities. Shaw, backed by the atheist and secularist leader, G. W. Foote, spoke against the proposal. He was a realist as well as a pacifist in his estimate of what would happen. He argued the futility of a further fracas and with his practised eloquence knew how to state his case. Caution prevailed. Some time afterwards Cunninghame Graham greatly amused Shaw by describing him as the first man to run away on Bloody Sunday. To this Shaw replied that he had been a fool ever to go to the Square and was now flattered by being credited with more sense than he had shown on that occasion.

Shaw's admiration of Charles Dickens for his exposure of the Victorian ruling class included the opinion that *Little Dorrit* is a more seditious book than *Das Kapital*. 'Though Dickens had come too soon to be a Marxian,' he wrote in 1947 in an introduction to *Great Expectations,* 'all over Europe men and women are being imprisoned in thousands for pamphlets and speeches which are to *Little Dorrit* as red pepper to dynamite.' (The victims of official persecution in that year, a point which Shaw forgot to mention, were some anti-Fascists in Spain and many more condemned for mere deviations from Communist orthodoxy in Russia and its satellite states.) Like Dickens, who found mobs on the march and threatening violence repulsive, as he showed in his description of riotous revolt in *The Old Curiosity Shop,* Shaw was no friend of the hot-heads who advised forcible measures.

Always anti-romantic, he could not sympathize with the romanticism of revolt which went to the head of G. K. Chesterton, his warm friend as well as frequent opponent in debate. Chesterton carried a sword-stick, which no man of such unmilitary bulk and clumsiness could ever have used to any purpose. He could not keep the imagery of blades, flashing and clashing, out of his poetry in which there was much cry of liberty. Oscar Wilde, who wrote with eloquence on *The Soul of Man Under Socialism,* in one of his sonnets praised the Christs 'who die upon the barricades' and then at the end said that

133

he was with them 'in some things'. The undefined limitation does not improve the lines, but it shows a reasonable caution. Shaw, who knew that barricades are a flimsy foundation for a new social order, was a 'some things' revolutionary when it came to methods of action.

When he was a platform speaker in the eighteen-eighties there was no Labour party but there was some Socialism in the air. At his death the Labour party had been in power in Britain for over six years; during the first five of those it had an overwhelming majority and was able to nationalize steel, railways, and road transport, and create a National Health Service. This led to fourteen years of Conservative government and to the realization by the Labour party that, in the opinion of the electors, enough of this was enough. Shaw did not live to see nationalization become such an ugly word that the Labour leaders began to use it sparingly and in the General Election of 1964 made it their objective only in the case of the steel industry. The safely vague term of social planning was found less likely to frighten voters.

The meetings at which Shaw in his thirties was so constant and so popular an orator were arranged by several kinds of organizing groups and societies. People who are at war with the world are usually in conflict with each other. The political left wing in democratic countries, where there is no iron discipline of dictatorship to gaol the deviators, are naturally prone to fission and the Socialists of the period were true to form in their creation of separate bodies. Liberty and equality might be the cry; fraternity went no further than the sentimental use of the word 'brother' to describe a comrade in the Cause, a habit which lingered on at Socialist and Trade Union Congresses even when disagreement was rampant.

The Marxian section was led by a member of the bourgeoisie, H. M. Hyndman, whose amply bearded presence gave the impression of an eminently respectable Victorian while he continued with small support to raise the Red Flag without despairing. In 1881 he had founded the Democratic Federation whose name was afterwards altered to that of the Social Democratic Federation. The title suggests a large union of allied groups, but there was nothing so big or so coherent in Hyndman's following. The S.D.F. was able, however, to maintain a weekly paper called *Justice* and several of its members made vain attempts to enter the House of Commons which must have cost money as well as effort.

William Morris, the founder and sustainer of the Socialist League which had a paper called *The Commonweal,* was at the head of another small group. The fact that Morris was an epic poet, a medievalist, and an expert in printing as well as in domestic furnishing and decoration has given some people the idea that his Socialism was only of the 'arty-crafty' kind. 'We want no dilettantes in our movement,' a later Labour leader was to say. But Morris was not a dilettante. He had studied the economics of capitalism while he was incensed by the ugliness of the world it was making. The fact that he was fascinated by the age of Chaucer as well as by that poet's writing did not interfere with his eagerness to promote Socialism in his time, to organize meetings and to call on Shaw, who had no romantic visions of a long-past Merrie England, to address them in his own idiom and with his own brand of revolutionary thinking. The life of Morris was full and, in the arts, fruitful, but his Socialist Leaguers were few and by the Labour Movement of the following century he was soon forgotten while the books issued by his Kelmscott Press were treasured by collectors.

The Christian Socialists were organized in the Guild of St Matthew and later in the Church Socialist League. The creator of and most influential worker for the Guild was the Rev. Stewart Headlam for whom Shaw spoke as a visiting sympathiser. Membership of the Guild he

William Morris

refused on the grounds of contrary or at least insufficient belief. Some clergymen of distinction, including Canon Scott Holland, eloquent in the pulpit, were either Socialists or favourable to the view that capitalism had created an un-Christian society which deserved the condemnation of the Church. The Rev. Conrad Noel of Thaxted was outspoken on the left wing of the clergy and several clerics joined the Fabian Society. The Rev. Percy Dearmer and Headlam were among these.

The activities of a Socialist parson in the East End are pictured in the home of Shaw's character in *Candida*, the Rev. James Mavor Morell, who reads Headlam's paper *The Church Reformer*. His secretary, Proserpine Garnett, reminds him of his immediate engagements as a speaker. Among suppliants for, and in most cases recipients of, his platform talents is the Hoxton Freedom Group. Its members are first dismissed as anarchists who ought to know better than ask for a clergyman on Sunday; but he will give them a week-night and cut a City dinner to do so. On the list are the Tower Hamlets Radical Club, the English Land Restoration League, the Independent Labour Party, and the Fabian Society. When his secretary protests that Morell is wasting his time on ignorant and penniless coster-mongers, Morell replies that they are all his near relatives. 'Relatives!' says Miss Garnett, aghast, and is told that we all have the same Father in Heaven. 'Oh, is that all', is her reply. It would be unfair to think that the self-centred Morell, so obtuse in the appreciation of his wife's contribution to his success, was based on Stewart Headlam. But *Candida* provides a vivid and plausible picture of the Socialism stirring in the sacred and profane corners of London life, corners which Shaw continually visited in his willingness to mount the humblest platform and give even the smallest audience his sparkling best.

In the north of England, Bradford was an early centre of Socialist activity. In 1891 Shaw was invited to stand for Parliament in the constituency of East Bradford; he refused with the suggestion that they should get a representative of the working class. Though a failed novelist and still little recognized as a journalist, his name as a

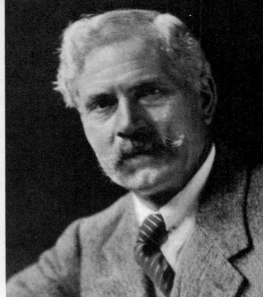

Keir Hardie   Ramsay MacDonald

speaker had been established outside London since he was ready to make long and tiring journeys in order to promote the cause. This was not altogether a labour of love and devotion. He never concealed his natural histrionic impulses or his pleasure in giving a performance. He enjoyed dealing with questioners and opposition; he knew that he could cope with them, and the applause which followed a neat and possibly devastating reply was appreciated and encouraged him to fill his diary with as many dates as did the much requested Morell.

A year after his rejection of Bradford's offer the Independent Labour party was founded there. Shaw shared with Keir Hardie the work of drafting its first programme. When the Labour party itself was formed in 1900, its first secretary was James Ramsay MacDonald, a young Scotsman from Lossiemouth who was a member of the I.L.P. The latter was a Socialist body in its propaganda though it did not carry that label. It remained on the left wing of the movement, but when the Labour party supported the Liberal government's action in joining the war in 1914 it was pacifist and enlarged its membership as a lonely rallying-point for those opposed to belligerence. Back in the eighteen-nineties there was no thought of a Europe in arms and disruption; the I.L.P.'s early policy was based on the familiar Socialist slogan, 'Educate, agitate, organise'.

One of its ablest members was a Yorkshireman from Keighley, Philip Snowden, later Lord Snowden; long afterwards, like Ramsay MacDonald, he swung over to the right wing during the economic crisis of 1931 and the formation of the Coalition government. Before he rose to be Chancellor of the Exchequer in the short-lived Labour administration of 1924, an office held again in 1930, he had been noted for sharpness of tongue as well as of mind. On a Socialist platform he could be as brilliantly bitter as Shaw was breezily brilliant. Shaw excelled in ridicule as well as direct attack; he did not seek to score a point with a snarl or a sneer.

A figure now little remembered but of great service to Socialism was Robert Blatchford. Born in 1851, he proved to be almost as good a Methuselist as Shaw himself since he lived to be ninety-three. His most active period was in the middle of his life when he had discovered a remarkable talent for simple, popular, and effective journalism. Thus he continued to make a living in the employment of the capitalist press after he had turned to battering capitalism with the ability of one who knew how to write directly for the ordinary man in his own words, instead of lecturing him from above in the jargon of economics and of Socialist theory. Blatchford had been a private soldier in the Dublin Fusiliers and he evidently did not resent the hard life of the army with its shilling-a-day remuneration. In 1914 he vehemently supported the war, and since many of his previous admirers were taking the I.L.P. and pacifist line his loyalty to the Socialist cause dwindled.

But he had done what the intellectuals had failed to do. He had stated the Socialist case in a human and often humorous way. When he founded and edited his weekly paper, *The Clarion,* in 1891, he enlisted contributors who shared his own understanding of what the proletarian would take in the way of propaganda. He knew that Socialist arguments would miss their mark with the millions unless they were made easily readable. His own short, stabbing sentences got home with those whom Fabian essays would never reach. He applied the same efficiency to the books which he wrote for his Clarion Press in Manchester: *Merrie England, Britain for the British,* and *God and My Neighbour.* The last of these hammered Christianity as hard as the two former hammered capitalism. Paper and printing were then so cheap that short books of this kind could be sold in quantity for threepence. He found a large market.

Blatchford also organized a corps of Clarion Scouts who travelled, often on bicycle, to carry the Socialist message as widely as possible. The present powerful Labour party in Britain owes its money to the trade unions, but its debt to the early speakers and writers was immense. While, at the end of the century, Shaw and H. G. Wells were capturing the young adults of the student class with plays, novels, pamphlets, and political books, Blatchford was doing the no less necessary work of making the product of the board school acquainted with and responsive to the Socialist creed. On unsophisticated minds the impact of his prose, a kind of tub-thumping in words, backed with enough statistical fact and a vibrant emotional force, was bound to be cogent. I can speak from my own experience. When I was at school we were ordered to write a prepared essay, that is one based on previous reading of recommended books. The Sixth Form master gave us Socialism as a subject and suggested, in addition to Shaw and Wells, anything by Blatchford. (This, incidentally, was in one of the public schools continually being denounced as nests of reactionary opinions.) I bought *Britain for the British* and *God and My Neighbour* with half a week's pocket-money and was immediately persuaded, or I might say verbally bludgeoned, into rejecting my previous political beliefs, which had been strong, and abandoning my religious ones, which had been shaky.

In 1881 an idealist called Davidson, who had gone to America after a university career in Aberdeen, founded in London a Fellowship of the New Life. Its purpose was 'the cultivation of a perfect character in each and all'. It was setting its goal high indeed. Some perfection

Havelock Ellis

may have been achieved among the Fellows, but no sudden change was to be seen in the outer world whose inhabitants they were to lead to such altitudes. But it was a period in which those of unusual or revolutionary views were few, isolated, and always happy to meet and to talk at length in gatherings of like-minded people, even if they were not inclined to join the suggested colony of secular saints and moral perfectionists in Brazil.

Davidson was able to collect some members of ability and with a variety of eminent careers ahead of them. There was Ramsay MacDonald, a future Prime Minister who did poorly in Downing Street but did at least get there. Another was Havelock Ellis, a pioneer in the psychology of sex and persecuted for his candid examination of the subject in all its phases, normal and abnormal, at a time when sex was treated as a matter for public silence and private story-telling of a salacious kind. There was also a noted humanitarian, Henry Salt, an Eton master who had made enough money to retire modestly to a country cottage and work for the prevention of cruelty to animals as well as to human beings. The Fellowship could be laughed at as a collection of cranks pursuing an impossible end since mankind in Britain or anywhere else is not likely to be redeemed and morally perfected by ethical discussions of the well-intended few. But on the political side the Fellowship fathered a notable child.

This was the Fabian Society to which Shaw gave so much of his time in committee and of his skill in pamphleteering. Those of the Fellowship who were more interested in social than in personal reformation met in January, 1884, and founded the Society with a curious name drawn from Roman history. In the war against Hannibal the general Quintus Fabius Maximus was appointed Dictator after the severe defeat of the Roman army at Lake Trasimene. His policy was to avoid further action, build up a new army with a new morale, and so with cautious delay wait for the right moment to strike. Hence came the phrase Fabian tactics. The Socialist wing of the Fellowship realized that the Movement could not be a gallop. There had to be accumulation of fact and penetration of opinion, especially the opinion of people with political influence. The thumping of tubs was not their form of exercise.

The Fabian pamphlets, to which Shaw was an early and important contributor, stated the case for the public ownership of the means of production, distribution, and exchange; the operation could be carried out either nationally or municipally. If anybody could put life into expounding and commending this policy it was he. Subsequently H. G. Wells was to state the Socialist case in books and articles which were sure to be vivacious. Wells joined the Fabians eighteen years after the foundation of the Society and did not stay in it for long. Policies of caution, diligence in committee work, and smooth co-operation with congenial colleagues were alien to his impatient and gusty genius. As a Fabian collaborator Shaw was equable as well as hard-working.

Wells wrote sarcastically of the Society's small and quiet meetings from whose petty deliberations he would emerge into the bustling enormity of commercial London. It seemed impossible to him that the hob-nobbing of this handful of earnest but unimpressive Tractarians with their 'dribble of activities' could have any effect on the monster they were proposing to put in Socialist harness. The fortress of Capitalism would not surrender to the petty methods and dilatory tactics in which the Fabians so innocently trusted. He did not remember that nearly all great movements have begun with the small stirrings of new thought. He did not foresee that those who were later to be called 'backroom boys' could be important in the winning of a war. He called on the Society to make itself much larger and speak much louder.

Accordingly he proposed the radical alteration of the policy statement known as the Fabian Basis with which intending members had to agree. When his demands for a bigger and better Fabianism were put forward and debated in 1906, he was defeated. He had stated his case poorly. The victory of the Old Gang, as the senior members were called, was chiefly brought about by Shaw's crushing superiority in debate. At fifty Shaw was in his prime as a platform technician and a debater who could knock Wells out of the ring. Wells was a friend, but far older friends were the principal Old Gangsters, Sidney and Beatrice Webb. The Society remained small, but its permeation of political opinion in the Liberal and Labour parties was continued in a quiet way.

There were new moves. A New Gang had to be considered and the incomers were admitted to what was called the Fabian Nursery in order that the young idea might be taught how to nationalize. Then a Fabian Research Department was formed to intensify the collection of factual ammunition. It is wrong to think of the senior membership as made up of dry-as-dust types. Granville-Barker, Shaw's colleague in the theatre, was one of the Committee. Just before the 1914 war G. D. H. Cole, who had been an active Socialist at Oxford, was particularly busy organizing and directing the Research section. His dynamic personality was not congenial to the Old Gang but they knew that he had great influence with potential recruits among his own generation.

Most influential of the veterans and extremely adroit in tactical manoeuvre was Sidney Webb, whose abilities Shaw admired beyond measure. Webb, Shaw's junior by three years, had gone from London

H. G. Wells in Bombay, en route to Australia

University to the lower division of the Civil Service. (As a surveyor of taxes he must have been a difficult watch-dog for tax-avoiders and evaders to circumvent.) Soon he was making enough outside office hours by his work as a journalist to give up his job and live as a publicist on political and economic matters. When in 1892 he married Beatrice Potter, the daughter of a prosperous northern family who had done well out of railways, her inheritance, not great but of a useful size then, enabled them to give their lives to the Fabian Society as well as to writing valuable books on industrial and economic history. They collected devotees and they knew where to find money for their causes. The recruitment of the wealthy Charlotte Payne-Townshend has already been mentioned.

Their contribution to the Labour Movement was that of the busy back-room until Sidney Webb decided to enter Parliament. He was given a safe seat, the Seaham division of Durham, and was its member from 1922 to 1929 when he was 'sent upstairs' to strengthen the tiny Labour representation in the House of Lords. He was twice given Cabinet rank, as President of the Board of Trade in 1924 and as the Secretary of State for the Colonies in 1930. Ability to address and hold the House of Commons, often a turbulent and ill-mannered audience, was not part of his competence. Unlike Shaw, he had never learned to speak at street-corners. Shaw would have been a much better parliamentarian if he could have endured the life, but having rejected the Bradford invitation he would not be a candidate for a place in a House whose performance he continually derided.

The Webbs seemed incapable of fatigue. 'The labour we delight in physics pain' might have been written over their desks. They collected good secretaries and worked them hard. Their home in Grosvenor Road was a hive of industry. The way in which they collected the rising people in politics was well described by Wells in his novel of 1911, *The New Macchiavelli*. There they were satirized, not too harshly, as Oscar and Altiora Bailey. Sidney never had his head off his work or his feet off the ground but Beatrice had an 'altiorist' side to her character and, having rejected the rationalism of her youth, had her years of faith, perhaps even of fancy, while the assemblage of facts for Fabians was the ground floor for Higher Thought.

Meanwhile Fabianism was pertinaciously burrowing its way into Westminster and Whitehall. Shaw's days on the portable platform of the open-air orator were past. His audience had become playgoers and readers of the middle class who enjoyed him as much for his wit as his message. But the fieldwork had to go on. Blatchford still put his Socialism into prose with a punch in it, the Clarion Scouts pedalled and preached, the I.L.P. was active, and the Labour party which had only been born in 1900 was soon confirming the old saying that 'union is strength' with the newly discovered support of Trade Union finance.

A Labour Representation Committee was formed in 1900 and this became the Labour party in 1906. Ramsay MacDonald was secretary of the first until it was transformed and of the second until 1912. For a while he combined this with Chairmanship of the I.L.P. Labour candidates had been standing before 1900. Keir Hardie had been Labour member for West Ham from 1892 to 1895. MacDonald endeavoured unsuccessfully to capture Southampton for Labour in

1895. Keir Hardie won the mining constituency of Merthyr Tydfil in 1900. At the General Election of 1906 there were twenty-nine Labour members returned. They were not necessarily Socialists, working rather on the left flank of the Liberal party. Their strength lay in the Trade Union funds behind them which were very necessary since Members of Parliament were not then paid any salary and could not have lived without their earnings as Union officials. When the Liberals decided that an M.P. was worth four hundred pounds a year the House of Commons was still a difficult place for a poor man from afar and with a London lodging to find. Its appeal was to those Labour men who had a safe Union job or who wanted position and reputation and could somehow pick up a living outside Parliament with their pens.

Naturally the first loyalty of most Labour members was to their Unions. Those who belonged to the I.L.P. were the principal intellectuals and supplied the debating power, while the Trade Union levies were the solid foundation of the Party funds. After the Great War Labour profited by the dissensions and divisions in the Liberal party as well as by the readiness of electors to consider proposals for nationalization and to be no longer terrified by the word Socialism. Labour was twice in office without commanding power and a drive for the kind of nationalization which Shaw wanted was impossible. Not until its sweeping victory in 1945 could the Attlee government make Socialism more than a talking-point.

Shaw, as a Socialist, was no enthusiast for the Labour party in its early years. He said that it 'made the House of Commons more and more an almshouse for retired Trade Union secretaries who call themselves Socialists only when they are told to, without knowing what the word means'. His vision was of a creeping paralysis on the Left caused partly by the limited Trade Union outlook of so many Labour members, partly by the extremely slow motion of Britain's parliamentary machinery, and partly by the tendency of the party system to impede any swift or strong action. That Bills have to go to the committee stage to be tidied up and made workable as Acts often means tardy progress, but it is a necessary way of doing things. Shaw complained that nothing is ever done at Westminster, which is scarcely true. Of Parliament in the nineteen-thirties he sarcastically remarked that not even the most timid Tories need be frightened of any relics of the Socialist faith since during and after the economic crisis of 1931 the Conservatives adopted MacDonald, the one-time intransigent Socialist, as their own puppet-leader. They knew, commented Shaw, that they could look after MacDonald better than he looked after Socialism.

This indictment was made in 1944. The achievements of the Attlee government of 1945 should by that time have altered his views about Parliament and the Labour party. Though an active member of the Society of Authors, an intellectuals' Trade Union vigilant in the defence of writers from exploitation, he disliked the idea of powerful corporations within the state. He included Trade Unions with the Church, the doctors, the lawyers, and the Stock Exchange when he protested against organizations which had their own rights of admission and exclusion and so 'would leave our livelihoods at the mercy of bodies over which we have no control'. A Labour party dominated by Trade Unions was not what he had in mind when in youth he toiled so indefatigably on platforms, when later on he became the enthusiastic Fabian pamphleteer, and finally when he was still inviting all to be Socialists without hesitations. What he meant by Socialism and its effect on the liberty of the citizen, for which cause he had marched from Clerkenwell to Trafalgar on Bloody Sunday, has now to be examined.

CHAPTER NINE

The Shavian State

BASIC elements in Shaw's political and economic thinking were his hatred of idleness and poverty. As to the first he complained that the Trade Unions devoted their efforts to harassing employers who, although they might be chiefly seeking profit for themselves, were at least getting things done. The industrialists, as we call them now, had to be industrious. It was absurd, he thought, for the Unions to be so much concerned with badgering busy men instead of joining with the Socialists to put the loafers out of their far from busy habits. John Tanner's Idle Rich Class must go. And so must the Idle Poor Class. When 'the workers' did not work, Shaw would have no mercy on them, provided that they were not being exploited. Their lives under his kind of Socialism would have been strenuous.

The other enemy was poverty. Instead of being commended as a stimulant of the spiritual life and a passport to heaven, it should be seen as a cause of general degradation, breeding despair of mind and disease of body in the slums and squalor of a penurious society and making inevitable an ignorant, abject, and unhealthy way of life. That is the gospel of Andrew Undershaft, the wealthy manufacturer of munitions in the play called *Major Barbara*. The Preface makes it plain that Shaw appreciated Undershaft's point of view. In argument with the daughter of a prosperous family who has joined the Salvation Army with a passionate zeal for saving souls the latter says that anybody can convert the hungry with a Bible in one hand and a slice of bread and treacle in the other. (The play was produced in 1905 when there was little thought of providing social security by national insurance, national assistance, and other state services and allowances;

MAJOR BARBARA, *Wyndham's, 1929*

the numerous unemployed had then only the bleak protection of a niggardly Poor Law.) Charity, said Undershaft, keeps the poor poor; it may claim to be saving souls but in fact it lets them rot in rotting bodies. The man who is hungry for a crust will not, when he gets the necessary bite, use his mind or cease to be demoralized in character. He can only think about the next bite.

As an employer of the new type Undershaft is completely different from the Dickensian Gradgrind and Bounderby. He demands good work for which he provides good wages, good conditions, and good homes. His men, he says, can nourish their minds and souls if they choose to, because their stomachs have been made reasonably full and their habitations made fit for civilized people. He has created round his factories the model town of Perivale St Andrews, 'almost smokeless, beautifully sited, and beautiful in itself'. That is his answer to Major Barbara with her talk of a common brotherhood for the children of one Father who is in Heaven. While she doles out bread and soup to keep the destitute from death's door she is more likely to perpetuate misery by her well-meant alleviation of distress.

With remarkable prescience Shaw anticipated the coming of a welfare state. In this case it is not made by politicians but by enlightened capitalists. The inflationary welfare state as developed in Britain during the last twenty years has been partly a political creation of the Labour party blown up with a whirlwind of paper money which becomes more and more plentiful while it buys less and less. It is also in part a creation of big business which has thriven on better organization, new techniques, and amalgamations which reduce wasteful competition but may also establish anti-social monopolies. The employers were heavily taxed to establish social security for the employed, but they were buying their own security at the same time. Undershaft would have understood the sense of that. He insisted that poor men are dangerous, adding that he was a dangerous youngster himself as he forced his way up from nowhere. As a result of his success he had ceased to be a menace and was kindly and beneficent instead. This, he said, is the way of most self-made millionaires.

Since Undershaft appeared on the Shavian stage we have had Hitler and the Communist commissars to confirm his warning of the peril to society when poverty is combined with a ruthless determination to win place and power. The welfare state has raised the rewards in the board rooms of industry quite as much as in the workshop. Now our Undershaft world has an abundance of plutocrats whose fortunes, not built on the sweated labour of sixty years ago, are, as Shaw said, such a burden to them that they endow gigantic trusts in order to get honourably rid of their millions by endowing medical and educational foundations and even including the arts in their munificence. This, it may be said, is charity over again, but it is a new and far better and more intelligent form of bounty, not the charity which, by doling and relief, continues the need for aid. One soup-kitchen only leads to another.

Shaw gave his skill in exposition to the stating of Undershaft's case. But his own policy would have nationalized the men's factories, left their owner one of the Idle Rich if there had been adequate compensation and a poor man (and so once more dangerous) if he had been expropriated. The Fabian Basis demanded 'the reorganization of society by the emancipation of Land and Industrial Capital from individual and class ownership and the vesting of them in the community for the general benefit'. The 'vesting' process, as practised by the Labour party when it nationalized mines, steel-making, and railways, allowed compensation. Its opponents in the Press used the short name of 'grab', but this 'emancipation' of capital was not robbery and the shareholders were not sent to the soup-kitchens for their next meal.

It cannot be said that Shaw was only a literary man at large in a world that he did not understand. Since he declined to stand for Parliament he had not been and never was involved in schemes for nationalization. But of municipal activities he had close experience and his small book, *The Commonsense of Municipal Trading*, published in 1904 and reissued with a new Preface in 1912, was based on his own labours in St Pancras where he was elected as a vestryman for the Progressive party in 1897. The local government of London was then divided between a superior body, the London County Council, formed in 1887 but merged in 1965 in the Greater London Council, and smaller local authorities called vestries which were later merged in the Borough Councils. The two parties contending for power were the Progressive party, Radical and to some extent, certainly in Shaw's case, Socialist, and the Municipal Reformers, Conservative and strongly opposed to municipal trading. Against the latter his book was formidably directed.

Shaw's service to St Pancras as a vestryman is well explained in St John Ervine's biography. He had got his place by what he would have called a job. When he stood for a seat there was no opposition because the Progressives were not putting up a candidate for another seat. He remained on the vestry until 1904 when he was defeated in an election which he made no conspicuous effort to win. Speaking smoothly to voters was no part of his principles or practice and the bitter campaigning against municipal trading was to put him out and the Conservatives in control of London's affairs for some time. He did not use his position in order to make clever Shavian speeches; he slogged away, of course unpaid, at the committee work which is the real core of local government.

It was a welcome change, he said, to turn from the foolish unreality of the fashionable theatres to the urgent reality of sewers and dust-carts. (He brilliantly remembered the dustmen when he invented the character of Doolittle in *Pygmalion*.) He served on five committees and gave them regular attendance and industrious attention. One of the subjects on which he worked was drainage and he was ahead of his time in demanding and getting public lavatories for women as well as men. Until then London had apparently regarded the weaker sex as so much stronger in inward continence as to need no 'comfort stations'. It was well for the stage, as well as for his own career, that he was put out of service by the electors of St Pancras and so released, at the age of forty-eight, for his work, and some of his best work, as a whole-time dramatist.

Readers of Shaw's writings about public affairs may well think that he, who so delighted in Ibsen's exposure of sham ideals in public and private life and followed his master by castigating romanticism in the theatre and wherever he met it, was himself a political romantic, little though he knew it and angrily as he would have rebuffed the suggestion. He attacked idealism as the mother of illusion. Did he not himself idealize the state? In 1887 William Morris reprinted in book form *The Dream of John Ball* which had been serialized in *The Commonweal*, the paper of his Socialist League. The great medievalist imagined the peasants' revolt of which the hedge-priest Ball was an eloquent leader proclaiming an age in which 'man shall help man and the saints in heaven shall be glad and fellowship shall be established in heaven and on the earth'. Shaw, as a Socialist and friend of Morris, must have read it and admired the beauty of its prose while remaining unimpressed by thoughts of fellowship in a saint-packed heaven, since he regarded immortality as a menace of eternal tedium and not as a source of eternal bliss.

In *The Dream of John Ball* there is idealism of the highest and Shaw would not be enraptured by that. But might he not in his own idealism of the secular state be entertaining a dream of John Ball in which the ruler is the man in a Socialist Whitehall, the Civil Servant omniscient and omnipotent? In that world there would be more discipline than fellowship, for Shaw was a strong believer in obedience for others provided that society was grounded on the Fabian Basis. Yet obeying orders would have been intolerable to one of his temperament. If, as a Labour Minister has said, the man in Whitehall knows best, Shaw would soon have decided that he knew better than the best and would accordingly go his own way. With his faith in the state, he idealized a social order in which he himself would soon have become the anarchist leader, if anarchists can ever permit themselves to be in any way led.

His Socialism was a perfectionist's dream. Everything done by the state, under Socialist tuition and guidance, would turn out wonderful. If the profit motive were removed and the administration of industry and trading were 'vested in the community', that is, handed over to the national and local governing bodies, a new efficiency was envisaged as though it were a certainty. It is curious that one who considered himself so acute a realist did not sufficiently, and at times scarcely at all, consider the nature of the new administrative personnel. They would not be supermen or a devoted collection of saints and sages. They would be officials earning a living, safely 'established', to use civil service language, and therefore, in the way of the world, ready to earn that living by following precedent, which is easy, and not straining themselves to be original or industrious beyond the usual standard of such work. Why should they become immediately more competent or feel a fresh and overwhelming loyalty to their employers, the public, unless the process of Creative Evolution had suddenly thrown up an unprecedented type of bureaucrat? Shaw never claimed for his creative Life Force that it worked rapidly or infallibly in producing human change.

When he did mention the staffing of a Socialist state he described the prevailing methods of civil service recruitment as contemptible and he did not bring forward any workable proposals for improving them. In 1944, after sixty years of advocating Socialism in national and municipal affairs, he ridiculed the various tests by which the repositories of power and bearers of great responsibility were chosen. These were the very people on whom the Shavian state would depend for its success and even its survival unless a race of super-civil-servants miraculously arose. Without examinations for entry to the service nepotism and jobbery are inevitable; these vices had been notorious at the time of Shaw's birth and he greatly admired the exposure of them by Dickens in his description of the Tite Barnacle family. Examinations there had to be, but of examinations Shaw had no opinion at all.

These tests, he wrote in *Everybody's Political What's What*, could be passed after coaching or cramming 'by any blockhead who has a good memory and has been broken in to school drudgery . . . The civil service excludes thinkers whose memories will not retain things not worth remembering and who cannot stomach school books, though their appetite for books which are works of art or helps to criticism of existing life may be insatiable. That is to say, it excludes the very people it should select. . . . These memory tests only enable teachers and scholars to be certified as proficient when they should have been certified as mentally defective.'

There might be intelligence tests; the fashion for these had set in before Shaw died. He described them as modish among psychologists. But he knew that many people who seem to have plenty of good sense fail completely in interviews and questionings of this kind. For himself he said, 'I have never yet come across an intelligence test that I could pass or an examination paper that I could fill up, except on a few questions my answers to which, being not the expected ones, would have secured my angry disqualification.'

He further mentioned the last word in the technique of sifting candidates; a person's physical equipment could be investigated as well as his capacity to remember irrelevant and trivial facts. There was talk, he wrote, of employing blood tests, endocrine tests, bacteriological tests, and electronic tests. He admitted some possibilities here, but his deep-rooted scepticism about the claims and pretentions of the men in the laboratories made him dismiss these specialists as useless. To him their experience was so fallacious as to render their discoveries mares' nests and their knowledge of political life was so superficial as to make them worthless assessors of capacity for public service. One so contemptuous of science could hardly accept its practitioners as preferable to the old-style examiners whose methods and choices he had deemed completely misleading as contributors to an efficient administrative machine.

When the state takes over an industry the workers mostly become the employees of a public corporation or board in which the property has been vested. They do not rank with those directly employed by the state, postal workers, for instance, as industrial civil servants. But that is what they really are though not so named. That they would become more contented and more amenable to reason in the case of trade disputes because they were now working for the community and not for private shareholders was an assumption of the early Socialists. It has been falsified by continual discontent on the British railways and among the employees of the London Transport Board which has a monopoly of the underground railways and omnibuses in the capital. The trouble spread to the Post Office and strikes have broken out in a department where there were none before.

That the state would be a perfect and beloved employer and that industrial peace would prevail was part of the Shavian optimism which I venture to call romantic. The dream was interrupted and nearly shattered when the Labour party realized that a comprehensive plan for nationalizing industries and making workers employees of the state was a serious handicap at elections and here was no bait for getting voters on the hook and into the Socialist bag. So, without abandoning altogether the drastic Socialist solution once accepted in Clause IV of the Labour party's statement of purpose, it was agreed that the British workers were increasingly disinclined to be ordered about by civil servants. This would have given great pain to Shaw, but his kind of Socialism, with his insistence on more work and no nonsense in the factories, would have been painful to the Trade

Unions. The state of his hopes was to be a hard master. He wrote that 'the Treasury offices should bear on their front not LIBERTY, EQUALITY, FRATERNITY, but NOTHING FOR NOTHING AND DAMNED LITTLE FOR A HALFPENNY'. (The choice of capitals for this slogan is his.)

The Civil Service has many strata and many varieties of ability and the lack of it. It has long been the target for facetious taunts about such Whitehall characters as Dilly and Dally and the Red-Tape-Worm. It has had at its head men of such quality that big business is eager to make take-over bids for their services. Salaries at the top had to be considerably raised in order to retain the men who mattered. The Labour government which took office in October, 1964, immediately created new departments in the belief that necessary action could thereby be accelerated and would not be frustrated by the usual bureaucratic methods, the passing of problems from one paper-loaded desk to another, and the inter-departmental disputes with their inevitable delays. On becoming Prime Minister in 1964, Mr Harold Wilson invented several new Ministries and thus multiplied the labours of bureaucracy and the already swollen numbers of the bureaucrats. Shaw would have watched this with more interest than confidence. There had always been a division in his ideas about the rescue of the country from capitalism. As a Socialist his view of the desirable ends was wholly at variance with his estimation of the executive means. He demanded that all power should pass to Whitehall while scoffing at the way in which it was staffed and unable to mention better ways of recruitment.

The politicians appointed to be Ministers have ample powers in theory to make the officials execute their policies. But they are enter-ing a new world, vaguely knowing what they want to be done but having to be told what can be done. They must take instruction from the men who have been coping for years with the tangle of intricate problems in their departments. The Minister comes fresh to the practice of administration and no sooner has he found his feet in one place than there is a 'Cabinet reshuffle' and he may be suddenly switched to a quite different throne, from agriculture, perhaps, to education or defence. The idea of the new broom makes attractive reading in the newspapers. The simple citizen looks happily for a wonderful spring-cleaning to follow. But the wielders of new brooms may be so much puzzled by the new job and therefore so much in the hands of the established officials that they can do no more than continue the sweeping of very old dust under very old carpets. From time to time a Minister may be appointed who has dynamic energy, no respect for traditional procedure, and a readiness to be heartily disliked by the stuffier members of his staff. Lord Beaverbrook fortunately achieved that kind of breakthrough in the case of aircraft production in the desperate year of 1940. Shaw knew how inactive state action can become and said so. Yet he was faithful to his vision of Socialism to the rescue.

Another of his repeated demands was for equality of incomes. All must be paid the same in his ideal society and all must work equally hard under threat of severe penalties, even the death penalty, if they prove incorrigibly idle and a burden to the community. But a state of equality, however desirable in a Utopia, has small attraction for the ordinary man and still less for his wife. It is true that ambition and the desire to get up and get on are not universal. There are those content with a safe job and an assured but slow rise in wage or salary as the years go by. But even these would think it intolerable that one who has just joined the staff should be as well paid as one who has been there for twenty or thirty years. Shaw's case for equality of incomes, though constantly and ingeniously argued, is such 'stuff as dreams are made on'.

He said of liberty in John Tanner's dream of a revolutionist's doctrine that most men are afraid of freedom because it imposes responsibility. There is some truth in that. But most men want the chance to earn more and, if they do not want it, they will hear about it in their homes. The so-called affluent society is full of people striving to be more affluent than their neighbours and of housewives who are fascinated by the new 'status symbols', represented in their

G.B.S.

case by the more lavish equipment of the home, the purchase of a car, and the recent addiction to holidays abroad. Majorca is finer than Margate to talk about on return. 'Bigger and better' is a cry which would have disgusted Shaw.

'Fair shares' is a slogan which is repeated without real belief. The 'status symbol' is its contradiction. The millions who place a regular stake in football pools or the Turf are hoping for shares as unfair as possible. G. K. Chesterton showed himself far more realistic than Shaw when he observed that the British are not interested in the equality of man. What does excite them, he added, is the inequality of horses. If he had said this later he could have included football teams and greyhounds and the luck in any lottery that is going. When Mr Macmillan introduced Premium Bonds he gave state sanction to one form of gambling and very popular it proved.

The Conservatives did not bother to join in argument with Shaw; they were content with the way things were going and would not waste time on replying to what they brushed aside as fantastic non-sense. But some Liberals did make a serious reply, especially Chesterton and Hilaire Belloc. The latter had entered the House of Commons in 1906 as Liberal member for one of the Salford divisions and was one of an overwhelming majority. Like Shaw he soon despaired of parliamentary democracy and of his party which he found to be as much dominated by money as were the Conservatives. Liberal or Tory, the old gang, whatever the label, were at their old games. The actors changed but the play did not. He summed up the Liberal triumph and its results in a brief epigram, *On a General Election*:

'The accursèd power which stands on Privilege

(And goes with Women, and Champagne and Bridge)

Broke—and Democracy resumed her reign:

(Which goes with Bridge, and Women and Champagne).'

Unlike Shaw he believed that the remedy lay with the restoration of the individual by the distribution of property instead of its nationalization by an all-powerful state. The dispute between the Socialist and the Individualist—Distributist was a term sometimes used—was argued in journalism as well as in books. As a boy I was an avid reader of a weekly paper called *The New Age* whose editor, A. R. Orage, had a remarkable knack of collecting men with deservedly big names to write for small money and often for no money at all. His contributors were free to say what they liked and knew that the readers, though few, were keen. Shaw and Wells came roaring in for Socialism.

Their opponent (I use the singular since Shaw described the Individualist animal as the Chester-Belloc) replied with enjoyable animation. Belloc published in 1912 a short book called *The Servile State* in which he maintained that the reforms advocated by the Socialists and Radicals would make a society in which the evils of capitalist industrialism would be perpetuated; the masses, having no property of their own, would be wage-slaves whether the boss was the old employer or the new combination of politicians and civil servants. Nationalization, if it came, would be more nominal than radical in its results. As Chesterton put it, the Duke of Sussex, if the land were nationalized, would become the salaried curator of state lands in Sussex. The farmer who might once have owned his own acres would have no acres and a mass of forms to fill up in order to satisfy the Duke's paper-chasing underlings, now civil servants.

William Morris looked back to the Middle Ages as an inspiration for his brand of Socialism. The Chester-Belloc looked back to the same period as a paradise of the property-owning peasant and as a guide to the necessary reconstruction of society. It was maintained that there cannot be freedom without private ownership and these individualists were passionate believers in the liberties in which Shaw had no interest. Freedom of speech he championed, but freedom to earn and keep money and to compete he regarded as fatally anti-social. Of personal possessions his John Tanner wrote, 'Property, said Proudhon, is theft. That is the only perfect truism that has been uttered on this subject.' Socialism, for Shaw, was a righteous theft to end theft. The clash of his views with those of the Distributists could not have been more complete.

There is no need to discuss here the much disputed interpretation of the medieval and Catholic way of life in Europe. Some assert that, when Belloc was being most vehement in his loyalty to the Faith, he was forgetting unpleasant facts. However right they may be, the Middle Ages were idealized because England was Roman Catholic, not yet corrupted by the Reformation and the pillage of Church lands encouraged by Henry VIII to the immense advantage of his favourites. To this upheaval Belloc in *The Servile State* attributed the start of a social calamity which was continued by the passing of power to the urban capitalists after the Industrial Revolution and the transformation of the populace into a proletariat. That word is derived from the Latin *proles* meaning offspring. The proletarians in Roman society were so called because their children were their only form of ownership. Belloc maintained that a man with no property, be he a townsman or a countryman, has nothing on which to fall back and therefore no bargaining power: in hard times he cannot make terms with his employer; he can only accept the terms his employer offers.

The success of the Trade Unions seems to contradict that, but their victories have come in a period of rising industrial output and full employment. A continuing and disastrous slump could alter this and put the proletarian back in his old position of having to get any work that he can and at the price imposed by a harshly competitive market. The Distributist kept thinking of the peasant with his own piece of tillage and his shared right to pasturing stock on common land. He may not greatly flourish, but he can survive and he is free. There are modern nations, said Belloc, when confronting Shavian Socialism, in which that kind of liberty lives on; he cited France and Ireland. What Shaw thought of the Irish rural system, its poverty, and its human products is set down in *John Bull's Other Island*; since then both the countries mentioned have considerably altered their way of life.

The Distributists argued, not convincingly even when the capitalist economy was far less massive than it is now, that there was still hope of recreating a free and self-determining populace. They had their own weekly journal, *The Eye Witness,* later *The New Witness,* to preach a creed directly opposed to that of *The New Statesman,* which had been started in 1913 with Shaw as one of its directors in order to present the Fabian case for state Socialism. The voice of the Chester-Belloc was small and crying out in a world where victory was going to the large. The economic changes brought bigger units and worked to the disadvantage of the little man on his own land or in his own shop and workshop, as Shaw well knew. Industry and commerce were thriving on amalgamations and the flood of new inventions demanded vastly increased outlay of capital for their development. How could the small man compete?

The Trade Union leaders took the economic trend of the twentieth century to be irresistible. They did not hope to end the proletarian status; they wanted only to improve wages and conditions. The rank and file were not interested in Socialist theory. The millions of members of the Unions and their wives had their eyes on the High

Street and its ever more attractive shops. They wanted and won spending money and they spent it.

The small minority employed on the land saw the advance of mechanized agriculture and extensive holdings. There was no future in the ownership of Starve-acre Farm with its run-down equipment, land in bad heart, and no resources. When in 1940 rich industrialists took up farming for tax-loss and tax-avoidance purposes, they brought in capital for renovation and machinery and bestowed some benefits on the rural economy while they amused themselves as new-model country gentlemen.

The old cry of 'Three acres and a cow', which incidentally had been raised by a Conservative, became futile. The trend was moving towards two thousand acres in the corn-growing land and a farm-garage well stocked with tractors and a combine-harvester. The age of the picturesque hay-wain had gone for ever. The farm labourer became a mechanic and later on the chicken-run became an egg-and-broiler forcing-machine; veal and beef were produced by factory methods. That is an odious England to many; it would have horrified the humanitarian Shaw. Whatever the ugliness of the new methods, they finished any chances Distributism may once have had, just as the huge industrial combinations had done in the towns. A great number of those who could be called the new house-owners held their premises on mortgage from banks and building societies and would not be free of their obligations for many years. The little man had large debts.

Another opposition to state control of industry came from the Guild Socialists who began campaigning against the policies of Shaw and the Fabians in the first decade of the century but had to abandon their theories in the nineteen-twenties. The word Guild suggests Morris and medievalism, wrongly in this case. The Guild Socialists accepted the Chester-Belloc criticism of nationalization. They agreed that it would not alter the status of the worker but merely substitute one master for another. They used the term Collectivism to describe the Socialism planned and run by civil servants. Their policy was a partnership between the state as owner of land and industry and the Trade Unions, transmuted into Industrial Guilds, which would be responsible for conducting industry as corporations within the state. This, it was claimed, would give the workers a pride and purpose in their lives which bureaucratic Collectivism denied them. Of course, the balance of power between the state, representing the community as consumer, and the Guilds, representing the producers, was difficult to devise. But elaborate plans for such a system with democratic control of the Guilds as well as of the state were drafted by G. D. H. Cole and William Mellor, and a National Guilds League was formed to promote the ideas to which they and others had given much time and thought.

It was a scheme that was ingenious but impractical. It made scarcely any appeal to the Trade Unions on whose enthusiastic support it depended. Their officials could not be bothered with such a complex proposition. They were sufficiently occupied with industrial bargaining and the application of pressure to raise wages and improve conditions and, if they heard of the Guild Socialists, they regarded them as nuisances with their heads in the foggiest of air. The mass of Trade Union members would have shied away from such a scheme if they had been aware of it. It meant making them responsible for the destiny of industry; they would have to apply serious thinking to its prosperity as well to maintaining its quality. That prospect could not have been welcome unless there was a revolutionary change in human nature. Shaw's statement about the common hatred of responsibility must always be remembered. Democratic controls, if they are to work, mean hard work. The Trade Unionist does not want to serve on committees when he has finished a day's work. The Guild Socialists were idealists romanticizing industrial democracy as Shaw romanticized the citizen of tomorrow as a devotee of equal pay for unequal labour.

The senior Fabians, dedicated to the cause of state Socialism centrally and officially controlled with some municipal Socialism on the fringe, were strongly opposed to a proposal of this kind. It drastically interfered with their long-cherished pattern of social reconstruction and, while Shaw cannot be described as a pattern-minded man, the Webbs were and he revered their judgment to an extent that has puzzled his readers. His hatred of corporations within the state has already been mentioned and here was a plan for multiplying such corporations and giving them an established and powerful position. The Old Gang had defeated the revolt of the turbulent H. G. Wells. They were not going to tolerate another breach of the peace. I was present at a combative Fabian Summer School beside the placid shores of Derwentwater at which the Guild Socialists, ably led by Cole who could be formidable, were countered by the still more formidable Shaw with the adroit Sidney Webb beside him. The Guildsmen were duly overcome and the Fabian policy was unaltered. The Guild propaganda continued but, without substantial Trade Union support, it was doomed. In vain was it emphasized that the Fabian Collectivism, so dear to Shaw, would only be a dreary replacement of capitalism.

Shaw did not live to see Socialism of whatever brand shelved by the Labour party, which retained, to appease its left wing, a threat of nationalization for those industries which 'failed the nation', a menace which could mean anything or nothing. Shaw would have been infuriated by this surrender to a reformist instead of a root-and-branch policy. He would not abandon his vision of the state as sole owner and administrator of the nation's land and capital with its subjects (subject is an apposite word in this case) doing the nation's work and directed by an élite of super-civil-servants about the discovery of whom he was deplorably vague. There would be no nonsense of one man, one vote. A diligent and disciplined people would have no more incentive than equality of income. The Idle Rich Class would have been painlessly liquidated, at least in the physical sense. The Idle Poor Class would have been taught to be industrious at the risk of their lives. The ownership of private property would have gone—so much for the Distributists!—and with it poverty of the worst kind would have vanished, too.

How much wealth there would be for all to share equally was not computed. Nor was the possibility of people being unable to relish or even to endure this regulated and flattened way of life. There are many who want to be less poor or even rich. These Shaw regarded as scoundrels and his writings suggest that there would be no difficulty in terminating the Acquisitive Society, as R. H. Tawney had called it in a widely read and influential book of that name. Shaw's equalitarian belief was a curious element in the faith of one who considered himself to be in all things realistic.

Protest meeting against Czar's visit, 1896

CHAPTER TEN

Things Believed

'I AM religious enough to have spent a great part of my life trying to clean up the heavily barnacled creeds and make them credible, believing, as I do, that Society cannot be held together without religion.' This statement occurs in the chapter called 'Religious Summary' in *Everybody's Political What's What* (1944). This, apart from the much shorter pieces in *Sixteen Self-Sketches,* was the last testament of Shaw's opinions about politics in the classical and widest sense, that is all that concerns the citizen, his civic conduct, and therefore his creed in general.

Here certainly is not the confession of an atheist. During his early years in London he had stood on atheist platforms, but he found many of the unbelievers to be as rigidly fundamentalist as the Bible Christians. He disappointed the hard-shell devotees of secularism. Merely to throw the Bible out of the window he found as foolish an exercise as insisting that every word of it was divinely inspired and that the Old Testament's tribal Jehovah was a universal Father in heaven. When asked about his creed he said that atheism was an empty reply since sensible folk want to know what people do believe and not what they do not believe. He disliked negations. A philosophy of life must have its affirmations with appropriate action to make faith effective. There should be no dogma without pragma, the word made into the deed. He moved on to his ideas of the Life Force, an immanent vitalism of the spirit. Materialism he rejected. His faith in creative evolution, through which the Life Force promoted change through choice, could fairly be called a religion.

Rationalism was a term which he criticized. None could have been more addicted to the use of reason in devising means and methods of action. But the end of action could not be determined by the same logical process. The material universe could be analysed by the men of science, but behind it was the mystery of life which intuition and imagination must help in apprehending. He would not, in his maturity, have objected to being called a mystic.

He continually emphasized his view that intellect is a passion and the use of it a pleasure far superior to physical and sensual delights. But he would not accept mental activity, however enjoyable and valuable, as the solvent of all questions about first and last things. In the Self-Sketch replying to queries about his religion he answered shortly and firmly, 'I was and still am a Vitalist, to whom vitality, though the hardest of hard facts, is still a mystery. I have to deal constantly in reason and with matter. But I am neither a Rationalist nor a Materialist.'

Shaw was once described as striding with a confident, unwearying step down the archway of the years. It was a very long colonnade through which he passed and its start was in a climate of opinion utterly different from that in which he died. He grew up in a country where the Protestant minority and the Roman Catholic majority, poles apart in their doctrines, agreed in one thing; both were confident that the other side would end in hell. Baptised as an infant member of the Protestant Episcopal Church of Ireland, he was never confirmed. His family's form of religion troubled them little; it was sufficient that it made them feel socially superior. Shaw confessed to a boyhood share in Irish Protestant snobbery, but as soon as he matured he despised the mutual hatreds and intolerances of the combatant Churches.

When he reached London he met a world in which the contention of the Christian sects was being complicated by the battle of the Christian faith with increasing doubt. Charles Darwin had published in 1859 his work on *The Origin of Species by Means of Natural Selection*. Evolution was not a new idea, but it was now powerfully supported with biological research. Darwin's book was of the kind called epoch-making and evoked much eloquent anger. Darwin, said the indignant believers in every word of the God-given Bible, was tearing up the Book of Genesis and making monkeys of mankind. But before this controversy broke out, Doubt and what was called the Higher Criticism were becoming fashionable among the intellectuals. A typical example was Arthur Hugh Clough, whose death was so finely lamented by Matthew Arnold, also to have his religious doubts, in his poem *Thyrsis*. Clough, holder of a Fellowship at Oriel College in Oxford, had been much attracted by Newman's High Church theology; but he turned to scepticism and in 1848 gave up his position at Oriel since the tenure of a Fellowship involved membership of the Anglican community.

The Church of England was fighting jealously to keep its grip on public life and on the universities in particular. Entrance to these academic enclaves was barred to Dissenters as well as other heretics. The Universities Act of 1854 supposedly opened the gates to the Nonconformists, but it was evaded by the governing bodies of many colleges. Unitarianism, which was described by Shaw as scepticism made respectable, was still deemed intolerable and a member of a Unitarian family, the young C. P. Scott, who was soon to become the famous editor of the *Manchester Guardian,* was turned down in 1865 by the first two Oxford colleges of his choice and had to enter one which possessed a tolerance still unusual. Doubt might be spreading, but the Church was not yielding to intellectual liberalism without a struggle.

The case of Bishop Colenso showed bigotry ready for unrelenting conflict. Born in 1814, John William Colenso had been a distinguished mathematician in his youth at Cambridge. He entered the Church and at the age of thirty-one was given a colonial bishopric, that of Natal. He turned from writing textbooks on arithmetic and algebra to theology and stated his disbelief in the doctrine of eternal punishment. His translation of St Paul's Epistle to the Romans with a commentary evoked a storm of protest. He had suggested that Moses was not the actual author of the Pentateuch and was denounced as a

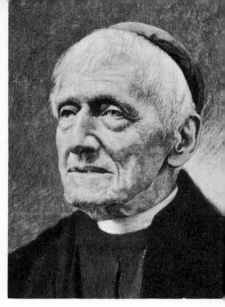

John William Colenso   *John Henry Newman*

heretic by the Anglican churchmen in both Houses of Convocation
in 1864. His superior in Africa, Bishop Gray of Cape Town, turned
him out of his see. The Privy Council nullified the deposition, but
the infuriated Gray hit back by excommunicating Colenso, a fact
later noted by Shaw as typical of the clerical Tite Barnacles.

The Church of England's war with its opponents and seceders had
to be fought on several fronts and these must be briefly charted if we
are to appreciate Shaw's analysis of Christian teachings made in the
Preface to *Androcles and the Lion,* a long and lucid exposition added
in 1915 to the brief and charming comedy about the early Christians
written in 1911. High Anglicans had been carrying their doctrine to
such altitude that some went over—or toppled over, as their Low
Church foes would have said—into Roman Catholicism. Even
Oxford, expected to be reliably conservative, was giving trouble.
The words 'papal aggression' were in the air, provoked by the
Pope's decision in 1850 to found Roman dioceses in Britain. At
Oriel not only had one of its best-known Fellows been lost to Doubt;
another and a greater member of its Senior Common Room had
been received into the Roman Catholic Church in 1845, a serious
Protestant casualty.

This was John Henry Newman, a High Churchman who in 1833 had published his *Tracts for the Times* and so given a strong impulse to what was called the Tractarian Movement. Of the Tractarians Macaulay said bitterly that they could combine the worst doctrines of the Church of Rome with the best benefices in the Church of England. This could not apply to Newman, a man of unquestioned integrity as well as profound scholarship, and soon to possess great influence. Thirty-four years later he was created a Cardinal; his secession had naturally given much assistance to the Roman cause.

There was a further distress for Conservative churchmen. This was a mild eruption of Christian Socialism in whose advocacy Charles Kingsley and Frederick Denison Maurice were prominent. Their belief that Christianity was incompatible with the great extremes of wealth and poverty and the rigid class divisions in Christian countries did not lead them into the theory and strategy of a vigorous class war. Their Socialism was of a pink and not a scarlet hue and was far removed from the robustly eloquent appeal to revolution made by the German exile, Karl Marx, and his friend Engels in their rousing Communist Manifesto of 1848. This was a call to arms in which the workers were reminded that they had all the world to win and nothing to lose but their chains. Their proclamations had only a small impact in England but were more effective in Europe where that year was marked by a wave of revolutionary upheavals. The mid-Victorian Christian Socialists were opposed to any such violence, but their desire to break through the Tory tradition and mingle religion with politics of the Left was an added and a serious annoyance to most Anglicans who now found themselves afflicted with the vision of 'papal aggression' on the one side and Socialist infiltration of parish pulpits on the other.

There had been philosophic Doubt; there came biological Darwinism. The Anglican Church was assailed, but could hold most of its ground stubbornly. Great men of science and able writers, such as Alfred Russel Wallace and Thomas Henry Huxley, explained and defended, amid outcries about intolerable heresy, the

Darwinian thesis. The champions of Christian orthodoxy were not clerics only. The Liberal statesman, Gladstone, brought his weight in argument and his authority·as a public figure much revered by his own party and also respected by those who detested his politics to the defence of the Faith. For him and his many followers 'the impregnable rock' of Holy Scripture was a fortress not to be surrendered. On the Conservative side Disraeli dismissed Darwinism by saying that he would rather be with the angels than the apes. There were points of theology hard to defend by the conservative theologians while wrestling with the unbelievers, but these were not viewed by the Church as barnacles to be chipped away. The Biblical Gibraltar was beleaguered, but its garrison would not yet capitulate.

Withdrawal to more easily defended positions had to come; the retreat was gradual but steady. The Anglicans could shrug off the popularity achieved in the first decade of this century by the Rev. R. J. Campbell of the City Temple, who was so much in demand as a preacher and also so good-looking that he achieved picture post-card status along with the favourite actors and actresses of the time. In his much-discussed teaching and much-read book called *The New Theology* he strove to reconcile the faith of the fathers with the doubt of the sons. It was complained that what he said might be new but was by no means theological, and more and more the modernists found in empty churches sufficient cause for a comprehensive revision of traditional beliefs. A century after the Colenso incident of 1863, in which year the rejection of Moses as an author and the refusal to believe in hell-fire as the eternal torment of the sinful had been made a heinous offence, the Anglican bishop of Woolwich published, without scandal and with no official rebuke from his hierarchy, his book called *Honest to God*. This dismissed the traditional doctrines of his Church frankly and drastically and had a very large sale. Shaw's chipping of the barnacles was in some ways rather less thorough than that which came from this handler of the chisel within the Anglican communion.

Unqualified declarations of atheism were nothing new. Shelley's

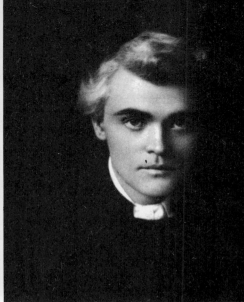

William Ewart Gladstone   Rev. R. J. Campbell

rejection of belief was almost joyfully repeated by Swinburne. There was no pale cast of sceptical thought in his 'Hymn to Proserpine' in *Songs and Ballads,* a volume published in 1865 and much reviled. Pallor was attributed by him to the other side in his raptures over pagan gods and goddesses. For him Christianity was dingy and a denial of life:

> 'Thou hast conquered, O pale Galilean; the world has grown grey from thy breath;
> We have drunken of things Lethean and fed on the fulness of death.'

Atheism was not of wide appeal to the mid-Victorian public, but it was organized for propagandist purposes by the National Secular Society whose leader, Charles Bradlaugh, was a powerful and courageous orator, much persecuted and stubbornly persisting. Shaw was once proposed for the Presidency of the Society, but he horrified its members by telling them that the Trinity was a reasonable union of Father, Son, and Spirit, that the Immaculate Conception need not be deemed absurd, since all conceptions are stainless, and that the adoration of the Madonna was a sensible addition to the

171

worship of the Father. This kind of talk, he said, froze the marrow in the atheists' bones.

He admired both the platform eloquence and the pertinacity of Bradlaugh who, together with Mrs Besant, was not only pelted with abuse but legally prosecuted in 1876 for advocating birth control. It says much for the sturdy spirit of the Northampton voters that they elected as their Member of Parliament in 1880 a man so harassed and traduced. On refusing to take the religious oath he was refused admission to the House of Commons and not in word alone. He was flung down its steps. Re-elected four times, he at last won his case for the right to 'affirm' instead of to swear in God's name and was allowed to take his seat in 1886. Many of the Secularists were individualists and Shaw, as a Socialist, was ready to speak against them and against Bradlaugh, too. But his loathing of intolerance made him an admirer of the Member for Northampton whose death in 1890 was caused, Shaw said, by exhaustion resulting from his long conflict with bigotry and obscurantism.

In the Preface to *Androcles and the Lion,* the four Gospels were closely examined and their differences noted. This was not done in a disparaging and destructive way; there was no claim that their considerable discrepancies should be used, as they often are by sceptics, to discredit completely the story which they tell. Shaw was not one of the school which reduced Jesus to a solar myth with the apostles attached as the twelve months of the year. Jesus was presented by him as a historical person and the Gospels were accepted as written within the lifetime of those who had known him, since the insistence on a speedy Second Coming would have been dropped if the record had been made when there had been no such reappearance. Shaw was not in the least worried by the miracles; dispute over these had in his opinion wasted the intellectual energies of sceptics and divines for generations on the assumption that the truth of Christianity was at stake. Rousseau had taken the miracles to be incredible credentials of a divine mission and said that, with them out of the way, the whole world would fall at the feet of Jesus Christ. This was dismissed

by Shaw as a nonsensical misreading of the Gospels. The trouble was
that millions have been much more concerned with the miracles,
which make comfortable reading for complacent people, than with
the message intended to discomfort and disturb them.

'Miracle' is a vague word and is used to cover exceptional healings
and events as well as those which seem to be impossible without some
supernatural magic at work. Subsequent accounts of the lives of saints
and heroes usually accumulate some such trimmings and they are
credited with legendary feats of a most unusual kind. The romantic
cravings of the simple multitude are satisfied and the stories, though
they may be worked up to impress the credulous, are not necessarily
a pack of lies. The life of Jesus may have been garnished by his
followers in the customary manner of over-enthusiastic disciples.
Shaw, however, accepted the abnormal powers of Jesus by which
were performed what could be called miracles. There is nothing
unnatural in faith-healing.

The point which Shaw emphasized was that Jesus took no pride in
these powers. He healed in compassion and not in order to justify
himself with signs and wonders. He rebuked those who asked him
to be a magician as well as a preacher. The rebuff was stern. As Shaw
put it, 'To be called "an evil and adulterous generation" merely for
asking a miracle worker to give an exhibition of his powers is rather
a startling experience. Mahomet, by the way, also lost his temper
when people asked him to perform miracles.' Jesus is seen as deeming
his capacities of this kind irrelevant and embarrassing. He believed
that he had come to advocate a new and radically better way of life
and had the sense to see that wonder-working was no way in which
to demonstrate the truth of a moral doctrine. 'To say "You should
love your enemies and to convince you of this I shall now proceed
to cure this gentleman of cataract" would have been to a man of
Jesus's intelligence the proposition of an idiot.' It is obvious that, if
the miracles could somehow be proved to be illusions or inventions
of the faithful, this would make no difference whatever to the lasting
value of the teaching which had to live by its own validity as an

ethical (and to Shaw a political and economic) call and challenge.

Man tends to make his heroes in his own image and to envisage his gods commanding what he already believes. During his life Shaw had seen enough of established and official Christianity in its arrogance, intolerance, and absurd doctrinal quarrels to be strongly anti-clerical. So he portrays Jesus as anti-clerical and few laymen will complain about that since there is abundant support for this opinion in Christ's conflict with the Jewish hierarchy. The Shavian line on politics and economics naturally led to his view of Jesus as a Socialist and, since there is Gospel advocacy of possessions shared in common, he could also be termed a Communist.

That label is now so widely and angrily flung about as a term of abuse that we must bear in mind its alteration of meaning by historical events. When Shaw wrote of Communism in his Preface to *Androcles and the Lion* and other works of his middle age there had been no Russian Revolution and to speak in favour of Communism did not imply commitment to a dictatorship by commissars miscalled 'a dictatorship of the proletariat' and enforced on subject nations by all the ruthless methods of a police state. This now formidable label he applied to quite mild measures of Collectivism which have been generally accepted by people of other parties. The Fabian Socialism which advocated national and municipal ownership and administration of the public services but did not include a general war on private enterprise was in some of his early writing called Communism.

In the Gospels he found much that could be so described before Marxist Communism swept across half the world and became a menace to the freedom of the rest. His Collectivist companions were not in the habit of waving the Red Flag or demanding a dictatorship of the proletariat. They did not mix easily or frequently with the manual workers and were much more eager to dictate to the proletariat than to accept proletarian dictation. But Shaw, contemptuous of mob-rule, was equally hostile to Mammon-rule and he strongly approved the attitude of Jesus to those who served Mammon, arguing that the Gospels contained the essentials of a wise and workable

ANDROCLES AND THE LION, *Winter Garden, 1934*

political economy.

While taking the Biblical accounts of what Jesus said as faithful to his teaching, Shaw did not remember that the strongest believers do not claim immediate authorship and allow a considerable interval between the death of Jesus and the writing of the Gospels. The apostles cannot have been shorthand reporters and must have been using a medley of quite distant memories of what had been said. In our times, even with speedy shorthand available, public speakers frequently complain of misinterpretation and protest 'that is not what I said'. Moreover anything translated from one language to another may acquire a different shade of meaning in the process. It is curious that people so often take a Bible text and argue over its implications as though Jesus had been speaking in English, and yesterday. What we have is an English translation of a Greek translation of words spoken long before in Aramaic, which the Oxford English Dictionary defines as 'the northern branch of the Semitic family of languages, including Syriac and Chaldee'.

This does not justify dismissal of the Gospels as wholly unsatisfactory evidence for the sayings of Jesus. His personality was obviously vivid and powerfully magnetic, and the doctrines preached were novel and arresting. The impact on followers and listeners must have been strong enough to make them easily borne in mind. Probably therefore the Gospels present a good general rendering of the beliefs and opinions of Jesus, but it is unreasonable to assume that every word in our English translations, of which there are now many, can be taken as completely accurate. Thus what Jesus said about economics is not as certainly known as Shaw thought when he claimed Jesus as a Socialist.

Accordingly, in removing barnacles from the rock of the New Testament, Shaw was by no means anxious to scrape away anything said about the use and distribution of wealth. Nor, as an anti-democrat, could he object to rendering unto Caesar that which was Caesar's since Caesar might become the governing body of a Socialist state. Where he did get to his cleansing and even demolishing work with the greatest energy and even ferocity was in the teaching of St Paul which he believed to be a drastic malversation (Shaw's own word) and indeed a destruction of the teaching of Jesus. The doctrine held to be most obnoxious was that of the Atonement.

Victorian Christianity was Low Church at the core. Converts were gradually passing over to Rome and the High Anglicans were attracting intellectuals and those who wanted more beauty in the Churches and more of colour and less of aridity in the conduct of a service. They disliked a ranting hell-fire preacher as much as that type of man disliked their rites and ceremonies. But the main body of belief was Puritanical and Evangelical. It emphasized the salvation of sinners by the supreme sacrifice of the Son of God. In the blood of the Lamb sinners could be washed, purified, redeemed from their guilt, and passed fit for heaven. Many of the Church's favourite hymns were insistent to a gruesome extent on purgation of this gory kind. These worshippers sang without repulsion of the fountain filled with blood drawn from Immanuel's veins. The wounds of Christ were vividly pictured: 'Hath He marks to lead me to him?' Outside the Anglican Churches the Salvationists were singing at street corners, 'What is it that makes me clean? Nothing but the blood of Jesus.' The Dissenters, with the fervid oratory of the pastors whom Dickens so fiercely satirized, were equally eloquent about the potency of the Cross on which the divine blood had been shed in order that the stains of sin might be completely washed away. To Shaw, as to Dickens, this Crosstianity, which he contrasted with Christianity, was immoral.

Shaw examined the history of sacrifice in the development of human belief. As soon as gods were thought of they were viewed as formidable, vigilant, and demanding figures. If angry, they had to be appeased. The simplest way in which simple minds could envisage this soothing process was by giving up something of value. It might be the finest animal in a precious herd. It might even be a son or a daughter. The idea of human sacrifice had occurred to the ancient Greeks. In the legend of the Trojan War Agamemnon was ready to put his daughter, Iphigenia, to death because the goddess Artemis, vexed about the killing of a stag, was denying his fleet favourable winds. The horror was averted and so was a similar homicide in the case of Abraham who was ready to have his son Isaac slain in order to avert the wrath of Jehovah. But there was no escape for Jepthah's daughter when her father, in order to wheedle divine aid for a victory in his war against the Ammonites, bribed Jehovah with the promise of human sacrifice. Having offered the life of the first person whom he met on return from his god-given triumph it was unfortunate that his own child should be earliest in greeting him. But, if the victim had been a servant, the story could not have been more repulsive. The tribal god of the Israelites was certainly to be written off in the Shavian scouring of the Scriptural rock.

In the Gospels, as Shaw conceived the message and purpose of Jesus, the crucifixion entirely transformed the primeval idea of appeasement by sacrifice. Jesus chose death because he could not withdraw the claim to his own divinity, a belief which may have come to him only at the end of his mission. He had no idea of atoning for the sins of all by one all-saving act of martyrdom. But, no sooner was he dead than the old idea of a sacrificial bargain crept back, and it was disastrously strengthened by the teaching of St Paul. This new and striking sacrifice could be interpreted as an atonement for the sins of Everyman who need only attest his belief and speak appropriate words of repentance.

Here, to put it crudely, was the bargain of all time, providing forgiveness without the tiresome necessity of reforming a guilty character or compensating for crimes committed. The guilty, in the reckoning of this theology, need make no sacrifice themselves. They had only to say that they had joined the faithful and to express their regret for past behaviour. 'There is no record,' wrote Shaw, 'of Christ's having ever said to any man "Go and sin as much as you like. You can put it all on me." He said "Sin no more" and insisted that he was putting up the standard of morality and that the righteousness of the Christian must exceed that of the Scribe and the Pharisee. The notion that he was shedding his blood in order that every petty cheat and adulterer and libertine might wallow in it and come out whiter than snow cannot be imputed to him on his own authority.'

Defenders of the idea of atonement will deny that this is a fair interpretation of what they believe. But the doctrine could be taken as offering an easy path to Paradise for those who chose to see it as a convenient method of evading responsibility for their old offences, however numerous and heinous. Shaw insisted that damage done must be followed by full compensation if that were possible. Debts of conduct must be paid and not written off because of that self-immolation whose purpose the Crosstians so conveniently misunderstood. A murdered man could not be brought back to life nor a mangled body restored to its health and vigour. In those cases a sense of guilt must be driven home. To punishment by imprisonment Shaw objected as a barren cruelty. For utterly useless members of society and incorrigibly bad citizens he recommended, inconsistently as most will think but without hesitation, a death sentence; this was to be carried out in the most humane manner. He had no belief in the sacredness of human life and deemed it preposterous for any to use those words who were ready to rely on lethal armaments to defend their country. He would have scorned the willingness of some to shelter behind bombs capable of destroying human and animal life across the globe while they were willing to call a murderer's life sacred and to be horrified at the idea of capital punishment.

This leads into ethical debate of a kind not to be followed here. The immediate point is that for Shaw Paul was the betrayer of Jesus because he went back to the doctrine of the old Adam who committed the first disobedience and so started the idea of original sin with salvation for all sinners through the vicarious sacrifice at Golgotha. When Jesus said of children that theirs is the kingdom of Heaven he was not regarding them as limbs of Satan born in original sin because of the offence of Adam and only rescuable by the shedding of blood on the cross. Jesus to Shaw was not the Saviour—men must save themselves—but the Challenger, who commanded them to live far better lives, devise far better policies, and turn their world from a vale of terror and tears into a community with shared possessions and peaceable practice. The rock of the Old Testament had to be de-barnacled by renouncing the barbarism of Jehovah and that of the New by going back to the words of Jesus instead of being misled by the fundamentally un-Christian teaching of Paul and his Crosstianity.

Shaw said that he could call himself an atheist only in so far as he totally rejected the tribal god of the Old Testament. He did not like the word agnostic because it was evasive. He refused to be called an evolutionist because that might put him among the Darwinians whose conclusions he detested since they were driving mind out of the world. There was, of course, evolution at work but to be acceptable it needed an explanatory adjective. 'And so,' he wrote, 'as Bergson is the established philosopher of my sect I set myself down as a Creative Evolutionist.'

Henri Bergson, by birth half a French Jew and half British, held the Chair of Philosophy at the Collège de France from 1900 until 1921 and was awarded a Nobel Prize for Literature in 1927. His book

L'Evolution Créatrice was published in 1907 and was widely read and discussed. It appealed very strongly to my own tutor in philosophy, A. D. Lindsay, who became Master of Balliol College at Oxford. Bergson, viewing the world as in a constant state of flux, an opinion as old as one of the earliest metaphysicians, the Greek Heraclitus, found in this universal mutability reason for rejecting mechanistic determinism and asserting the freedom of the human will. What Shaw and others had called the Life Force he termed *Élan Vital*. The cosmic energy was held to be as much in our selves as in the essence of the universe. There could thus be purpose in the development of species and purpose executed with energy in the onward course of man. That is the Shavian doctrine, derived first from Samuel Butler and other critics of Darwinism and confirmed by Bergson's thinking. This view was to be expounded in *Back to Methuselah* with particular emphasis on man's ability to determine the length as well as the use of his life.

Shaw knew that this was not a religion with an appeal to the ordinary person. He was a realist in his survey of life and knew that unphilosophic persons will not abandon the idealism, even the romanticism, of religious beliefs with their attendant myths and legends. If religion be something not ourselves which makes for righteousness or 'morality touched by emotion', as Matthew Arnold defined it, then it was acceptable if its brand of righteousness and morality were of the kind that Shaw approved, a goodness of goods fairly distributed, humanity in treatment of others, and freedom in thought and conduct so long as behaviour was not demonstrably anti-social. Jesus had been one of the world's teachers in whom the Life Force had produced an *élan* of the spirit. If to believe that is to be a Christian, then Shaw could be called a Christian and accordingly he was an outcast from the atheists with whom he had mingled as a young man. He complained of these free thinkers that their minds were by no means at liberty. They were enslaved to the kind of science which he castigated for 'flourishing childish amateur statistics as recklessly as the Fundamentalists flourished what they call Christian

Evidence'. The blind faith of the laboratories had to be rid of its barnacles quite as much as the creed of Victorian Christianity.

He did not expect any immediate change in human nature. The Methuselist paradise of mind triumphant is set away a long way off. In the meantime accepted religion could serve, even with its hideous menace of eternal punishment. Men might be advantageously frightened out of their vices. Here is one of his summings-up:

'I do not forget the warning of Jesus that if we try to clear established religions of their weeds we may pull up the wheat as well and leave the husbandmen without any religion. I detest the doctrine of the Atonement, holding that ladies and gentlemen cannot as such possibly allow anyone else to expiate their sins by suffering a cruel death. But I know as a hard fact that Methodism, which is saturated with this abhorrent superstition, changed our colliers and their wives and mothers from savages into comparatively civilized beings; and that any attempt to convert them to Creative Evolution would have made them more dangerous savages than ever, with no scruples, no personal god (the only sort of God they could believe in), and no fear of hell to restrain them. To change a credulous peasantry to a sceptical one by inculcating a negative atheism plus a science beyond the reaches of their brains may make an end of civilisation, not for the first time.' (*Sixteen Self-Sketches*, p. 79)

Before the atom bomb was invented he had seen the possible end of man who, he believed, might through his own follies go the way of the dinosaurs. Yet life might be indestructible. To creative evolution he saw no end; working by trial and error, the Life Force would have to improve on its first experiment with the creature so optimistically called *Homo sapiens*. Meanwhile man could plod on. 'Defeatism is the wretchedest of policies.' In that faith he died.

CHAPTER ELEVEN

Achievement

FROM the age of forty onwards Shaw was first much spoken about by the few and then much admired and discussed by a rapidly growing public. After this lighting-up time had arrived he was beset by those wanting his opinion on all sorts of subjects. He was interviewed, paragraphed, and photographed. What he did or said was news. Much of that he enjoyed. But what he cared about most was not the press cuttings but the preaching. He had striven to put forward his views about the improvement of the human condition. His achievement must therefore be judged mainly by his victories and defeats in persuasion.

To make money must be a satisfaction even to those who are not much interested in that kind of accumulation. Shaw acquired the income of a very rich man with none of a rich man's tastes. He did not house himself in spacious luxury; he did not buy 'period' furniture at great price or spend thousands of pounds on old or new masters in painting, now the prestige tokens of the rich. At the end of his life he raged against the war-time taxation which annually stripped him of most of his vast earnings. But if he had been able to keep far more he would only have had to worry about more ways of getting rid of it.

The theatre and its subsidiary profits were the main source of his wealth, which was a burden, and of his work, which was a pleasure. He wanted to make playgoing the recreation of more intelligent and serious-minded people and to substitute argument on large matters for idle entertainment based on trivial themes. To some extent he succeeded. It is true that his later and most argumentative plays were

never as popular as the earlier ones in which he mingled more entertainment with less instruction. But he had opened the way for a new
drama which discussed social issues and made it impossible for the
playgoer to leave his brains with his hat and coat in the cloakroom
when he entered a theatre. A number of new writers would have had
little or no chance if Shaw had not been a pioneer in showing that a
'problem play' could drive into issues of genuine public importance
as well as into the tangles of private and unimportant sexual intrigues.

His campaign against the uncritical raptures of Shakespeare-
worship was healthy since revaluations of the classics and accepted
masters must be made from time to time. The bardolatry evoked by
the Shakespeare quatercentenary of 1964 was in most of its examples
more intelligent and percipient than the laudations and celebrations
would have been in the eighteen-nineties when Shaw was alone in
challenging the value of the Shakespeare cult. His attack on productions overloaded with scenery and neglectful, even destructive, of
the text has proved effective. We no longer bury Shakespeare in
canvas nor do we mutilate the writing of a genius because we think
we know better.

New producers may be over-whimsical and even foolish and futile
in their efforts to find a novel approach, but the study of Shakespeare
by the scholars now considers closely and often fruitfully the life and
methods of a working dramatist, who was also a supreme master of
words, instead of immoderately worshipping the poet and forgetting
Shakespeare the actor with his parts to learn and plays to rehearse
amid the business of management. Shaw cleared away the empty and
gaseous idolatry and left room for intelligent appreciation. Whenever
Shakespeare is now properly acted and sensibly enjoyed there is a debt
to Shaw as well as to William Poel, Granville-Barker, and all those
subsequent producers who approached the Bard with a critical regard
instead of grovelling in adulation.

It is ironic that Shaw's greatest popular success in the theatre came
from musical comedy. Early in this century, *Arms and the Man* was
turned into *The Chocolate Soldier* in Germany without his permission.

It had an attractive musical score by Oscar Strauss with a captivating waltz-tune in the style of the period. It was hardly the glass of champagne for Shaw, but it was widely played and ran for three-quarters of a year in London in 1910. That was a tiny triumph compared with the many years of packed houses in New York, London, and across the world won by the musical version of *Pygmalion* called *My Fair Lady*.

Shaw left the control of his writings to the Public Trustee who maintains a careful watch on the uses to which his texts may be put by eager adapters and exploiters. The Trustee, consulting theatrical and literary authorities, vetoes anything to which it is thought that Shaw would have objected as misrepresenting his opinions. No offence was found in Alan Jay Lerner's handling of *Pygmalion,* which retains a great deal of Shaw in the script and even in the songs. The music by Frederick Loewe caught the ear of the world; it was in tune with the text and was not of a kind to make Shaw's ghost angrily join the traditional spectre who is supposed to haunt Drury Lane.

Shaw left just over one hundred and twenty thousand pounds. His total net estate had been valued at over three hundred thousand but British death duties took more than half of that. Not long before his end he had denounced death duties because they seized capital and allowed governments to squander it as income. Such taxation, he wrote in *Everybody's Political What's What* (p. 101), is 'wrecking the capitalist system on which civilization is still largely depending'. These seem curious words for a Socialist, but the operative word is 'still'. Civilization, he had claimed, would be preserved by equalizing incomes. If that were carried out, there would be no great estates to plunder. If he had died long after he did, it is likely that the death duties would still have been there and governments no less eager to spend the proceeds. No Shavian victory was likely in that quarter.

He, who had earned almost nothing in his twenties, had made money in plenty. He had been quietly charitable and the idea that he was mean is a false one, probably due to the fact that he did not publicize his generosities. He left personal bequests in his will. He died a widower with no children. What was he to achieve for posterity in the disposal of property? Profoundly interested in the English language, its spelling and its pronunciation, his first wish was to improve it with a new and larger alphabet. This he believed to be logical; he also thought it would save labour and space in the use of paper. His bequest for this reform was disputed in law and legally barred as impractical. Such a possibility he had foreseen. There were other legatees named in case this occurred. If he could not do what he wanted to do for the language he had used so well, he would remember the institutions which had helped him in his career.

His estate was therefore divided between the Irish National Picture Gallery in Dublin where as a youngster he had educated as well as enjoyed himself, the British Museum, another of his resorts for self-instruction and also his free public library during the early penurious years in London, and the Royal Academy of Dramatic Art since many players later to be his gifted spokesmen and interpreters had been schooled there. It is strange that he left nothing to any political cause, but his old associates of the Fabian Society were gone and he had given them invaluable help for many years. It was fair to decide that Socialism was no longer a youth to be helped with a student's allowance. It was now a faith capable of self-maintenance and he had assisted at its growth and maturing. So he preferred to make cultural bequests. To these legacies have been added his share of the gigantic royalties earned by *My Fair Lady*. It has been a large and substantial addition to the institutions which he wished to sustain.

There is a further irony in this. Shaw had dealt a severe blow to the romantic theatre which he despised; but that kind of drama is unlikely ever to perish. Shaw knew that and was not setting out to destroy the indestructible. He wanted to supply the necessary alterations. His young disciples in the audience and the bookshop were made ready for much sterner things. But in writing *Pygmalion* he had used the most frequent and favoured theme of the writers of romance, the poor girl exalted, the unfailing Cinderella story. It is true that in the postscript to the play he married the street flower-

PYGMALION,
His Majesty's, 1914

seller, Eliza Doolittle, to that not very capable gentleman, Freddy
Hill, and not to her tutor in polite speech and behaviour, Professor
Higgins. Mr and Mrs Hill are imagined as set up in a modest way of
business as florists and greengrocers.

But Eliza is made aware that the feelings of Higgins are 'deeper
than the infatuation of commoner souls'. We are told that she is not
only interested in him but even has 'secret mischievous moments' in
which she wishes that she could get him alone on a desert island,
drag him off his pedestal, and see him 'making love like any common
man'. Shaw's idea of her future did not allow that to happen in fact,
but he had given the hint of romance justifiably taken in the musical
piece but not sentimentally abused. It remained for Rex Harrison,
an admirable Higgins on the stage, to recreate the character with the
enchanting Audrey Hepburn as Eliza on the screen, and so to win
yet another victory for Cinderella and also for the legatees, whom
Shaw had blessed in this very practical form.

His political theories were partly realized in practice and partly of a
kind that could never be realized. Intensely optimistic in his belief

that equality of income would bring equality of happiness, he was so pessimistic in his view of democracy that during the nineteen-thirties he visualized dictatorship as an endurable and even desirable alternative. No realist can possibly hold the view that one person, one vote means that elections will be contests of pure reason, with rational programmes rationally argued. That confidence did to some extent exist among his associates and followers in the years before the 1914 war. The young Radicals and Socialists did then believe that they had only to put and keep in office a progressive party which would deal strongly with the House of Lords, still misusing its powers in a shockingly partisan way, and drive ahead with social reform. Thus democracy would become a workable and sensible way of government. That prospect depended on a rapid expansion of education to all classes, old as well as young. The Workers' Educational Association had admirable leadership from William Temple, later to be Archbishop of York and Canterbury, R. H. Tawney, Arthur Greenwood, who was to be a Labour Cabinet Minister, and men of similar sympathies. How bright the future seemed. But the Fabian, Graham Wallas, who was a political realist in his observation as well as a political theorist on the lecturer's dais, had to write a warning against the faith in reason widely spread. His book called *Human Nature in Politics* was to remind his fellow pro-gressives that the ordinary voter is naturally self-regarding in his desires, swayed by emotions, disinclined for hard thinking, and so an easy victim for the candidate who made promises beyond all possible performance and for the slick inventors of party catchwords.

It was a period in which modern Utopias were not thought absurd. A generation later, after the shattering effect of two vast wars on such faith in the human animal and his future, George Orwell produced his vision of 1984. He spoke of things to come with sardonic despair. He wrote in the mood of an age which had seen vast nations spell-bound by the Great Leader and then willingly put in chains when he had finished putting reason to sleep.

Whatever Shaw believed in his early years of Socialist propaganda, he totally rejected democratic optimism later on and went back from belief in man to a rather hazy dream of the superman who was to be at length provided by creative evolution. How this rule of intelligence was to be instituted within a reasonable time, with the rule of a super-fraud and super-bully avoided, he could not persuasively explain; what he could do was anatomize the folly of submitting authority to a majority of fools. He would not allow that the benevolent dictatorship of an unselfish and humane genius is a dream beyond any hope of realization. He could not agree with the idea which sensible people have come to accept today, that democracy is a poor way of choosing rulers but not so pestilent as the other ways of government known to mankind.

Autocracy, which he believed to be preferable to democracy, now holds the world from East Germany to the far verge of China in its grip and seems to have a considerable future elsewhere, not least in 'liberated' Africa. But Shaw could not approve of suppression of opinion, however much he insisted on Socialism based on social discipline. Yet, while he dismissed democratic methods as absurd he unreasonably approved of dictatorship as a form of delivery from political nonsense. Here and there his Socialism had its achievements. It gave him the National Health Service which he thought was the answer to the plutocratic medicine of Harley Street and the poverty and frustration of the Blenkinsops, the practitioners in Mean Street.

An object of his youngest wrath had been British rule in Ireland and he saw John Bull ejected from the south, west, and centre of his other island. His continuing dream of a Socialist Britain was to fade after his death when the Labour party had realized that even their own supporters were beginning to think it a nightmare and were preferring co-operation with reformed capitalism to the service of the state as a universal employer. Probably not many Communists are aware that Lenin wrote a tract for his time called *Infantile Diseases of the Left Wing* and it must be admitted that Shaw was a victim of that kind of infection in his propagandist dream and remained susceptible to recurrent attacks. Some of his political writing seems elementary in its conceptions of things possible and practical. But it is only fair to his theories of the state to remember that he began his thinking about Socialism in a world whose economy was quite different from our own and much simpler.

The structure of productive and commercial organization was less complicated and so were the techniques of productive industry. In the Victorian world other nations were learning from Britain the use of the machinery which she exported to these ready pupils, thus creating the quick-minded competitors who would, like the Japanese, soon be pouring the products of their very cheap labour into the British market. How was a Socialist nation, with high wages, to meet that rivalry? Alterations in the nature of trade and of social ranking were to sweep past the authors of the Fabian tracts.

Technology is an imposing word, but to mouth it proudly in the manner of the nineteen-sixties does not solve all problems. The Labour party, to keep itself up-to-date, is eloquent on the subject. Shaw as a Socialist knew little of it though he was interested in such inventions as the motor-car, of which he was an early and audacious driver. He began his thinking in terms of social justice in the age of the horse, not of industry compelled to fight for its prosperity and even for survival in a mechanized and automated society with new wonders of electronic contrivance announced almost daily.

Since his time we have developed a new language of economic development. There has been the rise of an Affluent Society, many of whose members see in Socialism more a menace of boredom than the old panacea. We hear too of a Managerial Society in which those who know how to run things have no wish to be overrun by civil servants. The use of back-sight is easy, and Shaw's thinking about capitalism and the state may be lightly dismissed today as the hallucinations of a deluded prophet. Properly to evaluate his political and economic hopes and claims we must bear in mind that they were formed and defended in the Britain of quill pens and not of computers.

It can always be said in Shaw's defence that, though he demanded impossible things and made insupportable claims on behalf of his simple cures for social ailments, he was never vague, never pompous, and never tedious. He did not write his prescriptions in Latin or wrap a remedy in a polysyllabic jargon. One of his lasting achievements was to apply an admirable style of writing to subjects whose present expositors are often so clumsy in their use of words as to make reading them a test of endurance. Political economy was never 'the dismal science' when Shaw was laying down his laws. To create an Undershaft was the dramatist's achievement; to present his opinions in a spritely Preface was the achievement of the pamphleteer.

Shaw was to see the position and payment of the medical profession altered in the way that he wanted. His own favourite means to private and public health, abstinence from meat, alcohol, and tobacco, have been little accepted. And yet the physical state of the nation has greatly improved and the laboratory chemists have made, along with some deplorable blunders, a notable series of therapeutic advances. The campaign against inoculation as a filthy and futile practice has been a failure. Shaw regarded the civic Medical Officers of Health as the best of a bad lot in his estimation of doctors. Is there one M.O.H. in the country who would abolish vaccination and refuse to immunize children against diphtheria?

Since the present generation has a better expectation of life than any of its predecessors, it ought, according to Shaw's Methuselist doctrine, to grow in wisdom: perhaps it will. It is true that longer experience of life in general and of the particular profession in which a man works should add to the value of the expert and make it seem absurd to force him into retirement when he has most knowledge of his subject. It can be replied that old minds tend to be closed minds and that the owner of knowledge gathered over the years may be stubbornly reluctant to accept a new invention or idea. It is partly for this reason that so many are pensioned at sixty or even earlier while they might still be vigorous and capable for ten or even twenty more good years.

Another cause for early retirements is the necessity for opening sufficient doors to the young. At the same time there is a sad waste of socially valuable abilities among the host of people still fit for good work and wanting to do it who have to fill their days with unpaid, irrelevant occupations and time-killing games which they may not enjoy. An Inspector of Schools once asked a boy what he was doing. He replied, 'It's my hobby. And I hate it.' One of the multitudinous inquirers who compile sociological reports might get the same answer from many of the active seniors who are left with nothing to do but amuse themselves. Shaw had little appetite for leisure and leisure enforced year after year would have been an inferno to him.

We cannot expect complete consistency in a man who lives for nearly a century with a restless, original, and unwearying mind, fluent with his pen, voluble on the platform, and determined to teach the world how to behave itself over a wide field of morals and manners. When Walt Whitman was accused of being a muddle-head who said one thing on this day and another on the next he replied, 'Do I contradict myself? Yes, I contradict myself. I am large. I contain multitudes.' Shaw could have made the same retort with more justification. If Dickens could be called a mob as well as a man, Shaw can similarly be described as the mixture of a brains trust and a mass meeting. He had begun as an Irishman and ended as a man of the universe.

There were divergencies of opinion. Let us admit them. In *The Revolutionist's Handbook* of John Tanner one of his maxims states, 'Every man over forty is a scoundrel.' This implies that at middle age we become conservative and obstructive. But in *Back to Methuselah* it is argued at length that only the wisdom of great age and its accumulated experience can save mankind. This is exemplified in the sagacity of the Ancients in the fifth section of his Pentateuch. We can take the former view as a sudden surrender to the temptation to make a startling remark and the latter as the considered judgment of Shaw in his sixties. A man who contains multitudes must be allowed to speak for all the moods of mental versatility.

His statements about education combine the admission that keeping order is essential with scathing attacks on the maintenance of discipline and on the disciplinarians who demand obedience as a necessity in the classroom. Marriage he regarded as a necessary institution for the maintenance of the race and rearing of families; but he said that it was only tolerable if easily terminated by divorce on the request of either party. In that case, what becomes of the family? His attitude to money mingled a policy of equal incomes with annoyance at high personal taxation. It is difficult to see how workers of unequal energy and quality can be kept level in rewards without confiscation of what the more productive man deserves and surely expects to earn.

In religion he abandoned his early atheism because he disliked a negative creed and preferred his Creative Evolution which was affirmative and optimistic. Christianity he championed for its equalitarianism. The saying that we are all sons of one Father was welcomed for that reason; yet, while he could fit that into his pattern of human progress, he denounced democracy as government by those wholly unfitted to govern and demanded the rule of the capable few. The Father, it seems, has a family most of whom are fools quite unequal to the wise minority. Shaw, if challenged on the deviations of his thinking, could have answered that he had given the world a clear enough picture of what he wanted in clear enough terms and that only a niggling critic would seek for total uniformity of views in so large a canon of Shavian scriptures.

What cannot be disputed is his immense impact on beliefs and opinions far and wide. This began when he was approaching middle age in years and was retaining all the *élan* of a young man in a hurry. His humanitarian passion and his hatred of cruelty were beyond dispute. It was said that he owed much of his doctrine to Nietzsche. This he denied, claiming that he drew much more on Bunyan's Christianity and Samuel Butler's anti-Darwinism than on any Germanic ideas of the superman advanced by the somewhat demented author of *Thus Spake Zarathustra*. G. K. Chesterton ended a jocose rhymed alphabet with these lines about the angry and dyspeptic Nietzsche,

'Z, Zarathustra who couldn't take stout,
He made war on the weak and they banged him about.'

Shaw, who also would not take stout, made war on the big battalions
and on the strength of things established and accepted. He banged
John Bull, who was no weakling. He banged prevailing notions or
superstitions, as he would have called them, which were so tenaciously
held that he was bound to be reviled for his audacious rebellion. On
the fringe of the unyielding many was a growing minority of those
who discovered that he was saying briefly and brilliantly what they
had been thinking and could not so effectively express. Shakespeare's
genius was to put into the best possible words what people feel or
have mutely in their minds. Shaw did the same service for the restless
and unsatisfied minority.

Gradually the complacent and conservative majority began to
listen because he had the good sense to approach them as Joey the
Clown who would make them take true words spoken in jest and
not as a Jack-in-the-Box who could only jump out and frighten
them. For the junior members of a 'stuffy family' he came in like a
whirlwind and shattered the tin gods of parental veneration. He was
not, like William Morris and Hilaire Belloc, recalling the Middle
Ages; he was giving shock treatment to the middle-aged.

In the Victorian and Edwardian home he acted as a vacuum-cleaner,
sucking up and expelling all the clutter and dust of stale traditions.
He was a window-opener and a window-cleaner; he tore down lace
curtains and exposed a new vista of the social scene. He achieved a
tremendous feat of ventilation. It can be said that he never saw the
realization of many of the reforms for which he had argued. But it
has been well remarked that 'the political idealist often does not get
what he asks for but does get what he wants'. In other words, the
general pressure of his thinking wins a large and dispersed result
while failing to get particular reforms. That was not said about
Shaw, but it does fairly summarize the Shavian achievement.

With the passing of decades it was bound to happen that, when the brisk young insurgent became the Grand Old Man, what had seemed so daring would dwindle to seeming tame. What more disastrous than to be taken for granted? The agitator who once was abused and shouted down is aware of the failure that awaits those to whom all men listen. Shaw pointed this out in the Preface to *Heartbreak House*, a play written during the 1914–18 War and published and staged soon after it. Before the War came the plays of Chekhov had been acted in London only before small audiences in occasional productions of the Stage Society. The intellectuals had murmured, 'How Russian!' Shaw thought, 'How European!' The plays seemed to him to fit the country houses in Britain as well as across the Channel.

Their comfortably placed owners were dabbling gently with the arts and thumbing books instead of indulging in the eating, drinking, flirting, and hunting of the Horseback Halls near by them. In London they might go to a Chekhov play and see themselves mirrored. But they, these charming dilettantes, were untouched. 'The same nice people, the same utter futility' was Shaw's comment when he compared the week-enders in their Heartbreak Houses with the feckless folk of the Russian dramatist. These literate and fairly informed gentry, he wrote, had social influence and could have done something to stop the drift and folly of what he called 'the wicked half-century' of late Victorian and Edwardian Britain. They had been warned by himself and his fellow writers, but they did nothing. They hated politics. They would not face urgent realities. On their shelves were the books of Arnold Bennett, H. G. Wells and John Galsworthy, and plays by Granville-Barker and himself. In a superficial way they were Shavians. In the only way that mattered they were not. They knew what he was saying, dismissed it as interesting or amusing, and took no further notice.

The success of the rebellious innovator is a species of failure when his novelties are no longer new. Shaw realized that when a challenging message is accepted the sting has been drawn. The history of Christianity was the most obvious example of that and as a particular instance he took the canonization of Saint Joan. Her enemies had cruelly destroyed her body. In repentance for that crime the Church, thinking to bless, destroyed her spirit. When she was made a Saint the Voices, which she heard and obeyed to the dismay of her superiors, were effectively silenced. 'Woe unto me when all men praise me' is one of the Maid's last speeches in the epilogue of Shaw's play. She knew what acceptance meant. So did her author when the world began to praise him.

CHAPTER TWELVE

The Shaw Years

IT is always difficult to say of an author's work when it was written since any book or play may have been in mind for a long time, begun, laid aside, and finished much later. *Heartbreak House* for example was begun in 1913 and not seen in London until 1920. Definite dates can only be given for publication or production. Many of Shaw's plays were staged in other countries before they could be seen in his own. For brevity and convenience only British productions are mentioned here. Full details are to be found in Maurice Colbourne's book, *The Real Bernard Shaw*.

1856 George Bernard Shaw born at 33 Synge Street, Dublin, July 26th. Oscar Fingal O'Flahertie Wills Wilde born in Dublin. Crimean War ends.

1857 The Queen's reign now twenty years old. The early Victorian period in British life is shifting to mid-Victorian. Charlotte Frances Townsend, later Payne-Townshend, later Mrs Bernard Shaw, born at Derry in Ireland, January 20th.

1859 Charles Darwin's *Origin of Species* published. Long controversy about evolution and natural selection begins.

1861 American Civil War. Death of the Prince Consort.

1866 H. G. Wells born. Fenians active in Ireland.

1867 Shaw sent to his first school in Dublin. *Das Kapital* by Karl Marx published.

1870 Education Act provides foundation for a national system of schooling in England and Wales.

1871 Shaw enters an estate agent's office in Dublin. Sees Henry

Karl Marx

Irving act the part of Digby Grant in *The Two Roses* and picks him out as 'an actor for me'.

1872　Shaw's mother and sisters move to London.

1876　Shaw leaves his work in Dublin and joins his mother in Fulham.

1879　Shaw briefly employed by the Edison Telephone Company. Joins Zetetical Society and becomes a speaker. Begins to meet Socialists and starts his life-long friendship with and admiration of Sidney Webb. Henry George's *Progress and Poverty* published.

1879/　Shaw writing but not finding a publisher for his novels,
　1881　*Immaturity, The Irrational Knot,* and *Love among the Artists.*

1881　Suffers from smallpox.

1882　Shaw hears Henry George speak and is much impressed.

1883　Death of Karl Marx. Fabian Society founded. Shaw meets and becomes friends with William Archer. His first love affair, Miss Alice Lockett is the lady.

1884　Much Socialist activity in London. Foundation of H. M.

Hyndman's Social Democratic Federation and William Morris's Socialist League. Shaw joins the Fabians.

1885 Shaw, with his mother, living at 29 Fitzroy Square. Gets work as a reviewer of books for the *Pall Mall Gazette*. Lectures on Socialism to the Zetetical Society and converts Mrs Annie Besant. Meets Mrs Jenny Patterson and Miss May Morris.

1886 Shaw busy with ill-paid journalism and unpaid platform speaking. Art critic for *The World,* to which he was introduced by William Archer. Charles Bradlaugh admitted to the House of Commons.

1887 'Bloody Sunday' in Trafalgar Square.

1888 Under the pseudonym of Cornetto di Basso, begins two years of musical criticism for *The Star*.

1889 First production of an Ibsen play in London, *A Doll's House,* at the Novelty Theatre with Janet Achurch as Nora. Shaw becomes increasingly the student and later champion and expositor of Ibsen.

Henrik Ibsen

1890   Shaw begins four years of musical criticism for *The World*. Delivers a lecture on Ibsen to the Fabian Society.

1891   Productions of Ibsen's *Rosmersholm* and *Hedda Gabler* in London. Private production of *Ghosts* by J. T. Grein's Independent Theatre. Shaw amplifies his Fabian lecture and publishes *The Quintessence of Ibsenism*.

1892   Independent Theatre produces *Widowers' Houses* for two performances at the Royalty Theatre. Sidney Webb marries Beatrice Potter.

1893   Shaw busy writing plays which had to await production.

1894   *Arms and the Man,* backed by Miss Annie Horniman, produced at the Avenue Theatre. Shaw ceases his writing for *The World*.

1895   Frank Harris appoints Shaw dramatic critic of *The Saturday Review,* in which position he remains four years, establishing a reputation for brilliance. He learns to ride a bicycle.

1896   Oscar Wilde sentenced to two years' imprisonment. Shaw meets Charlotte Payne-Townshend who becomes a member of the Fabian Society.

1897   Shaw becomes a vestryman of St Pancras. *The Man of Destiny* produced at Croydon. *The Devil's Disciple* successfully produced by Richard Mansfield in New York. The author, receiving eight hundred and fifty pounds in royalties, says, 'I am a man of wealth.'

1898   Shaw ill with a poisoned foot. Resigns from *The Saturday Review* and marries Charlotte Payne-Townshend. Recuperates in Surrey. Begins to publish his plays.

1899   Stage Society and Irish Literary Theatre founded. Stage Society produces *You Never Can Tell*.

1900   The Shaws move to Adelphi Terrace, their home for twenty-seven years. The Stage Society produces *Captain Brassbound's Conversion*.

1901   Death of Queen Victoria.

1902   End of Boer War. *Mrs Warren's Profession* produced by the

Stage Society, which, being a playgoers' limited society, could offer their members work banned by the Censor.

1903   Shaw resigns from St Pancras Borough Council, the new title of the previous Vestry. H. G. Wells joins the Fabians.

1904   Shaw stands unsuccessfully as a Progressive for the London County Council. Defends Municipal Socialism in a short book, *The Commonsense of Municipal Trading*. Granville-Barker starts producing for the Vedrenne-Barker seasons at the Royal Court Theatre. *John Bull's Other Island* staged there.

1905   The country house at Ayot St Lawrence bought. *Man and Superman* and *Major Barbara* produced at the Royal Court Theatre. Death of Sir Henry Irving.

1906   General Election. Overwhelming victory of the Liberal party. Strife with Wells in the Fabian Society. *The Doctor's Dilemma* produced at the Court Theatre. Ellen Terry appears as Lady Cecily Waynflete in *Captain Brassbound's Conversion*. Shaw sits for sculpture by Rodin.

THE DOCTOR'S DILEMMA, *Haymarket, 1942*

1907   *Caesar and Cleopatra,* written nine years earlier, produced by Forbes Robertson at the Savoy Theatre.

1908   Publishes short book on *The Sanity of Art,* included in Major Critical Essays, Standard Edition.

1909   *The Showing Up of Blanco Posnet,* banned by the Censor in England, produced at the Abbey Theatre, Dublin. Shaw contributes his statement on the Censorship to Joint Parliamentary Committee appointed to report on the working of the Censorship.

1910   Death of King Edward VII. Charles Frohman starts repertory season at the Duke of York's. The programme included Shaw's *Misalliance* and John Galsworthy's *Justice. The Dark Lady of the Sonnets* produced at a matinée in aid of the proposed National Theatre.

1911   *Fanny's First Play* produced at the Little Theatre. Proves exceptionally popular, moves to the Kingsway Theatre in 1913, and has 624 performances in all.

1913   *Androcles and the Lion* produced at the St James's Theatre. Additions made to a new edition of *The Quintessence of Ibsenism. Great Catherine* produced at the Vaudeville Theatre. Death of Shaw's mother.

1914   *Pygmalion* produced in April by Sir Herbert Beerbohm Tree at His Majesty's Theatre. First World War begins on August 4th. In November Shaw writes *Commonsense about the War* as a supplement to the *New Statesman,* subsequently issued as a pamphlet.

1916   Asquith's government replaced by a Coalition with Lloyd George as Prime Minister. Abortive attempt to overthrow English rule in Dublin. With serious theatrical activity abandoned, Shaw writes some short, light plays, two of which, *O'Flaherty V.C.* and *Augustus Does His Bit* are produced in the following year.

1917   Shaw visits Western Front. Russian Revolutions. Kerensky's moderate government set up in February and overthrown by

Lenin and the Bolshevik Communists in October. Death of Sir Herbert Tree.

1918 First measure of Votes for Women becomes law. End of war.

1920 League of Nations formed.

1921 *Heartbreak House* produced at the Royal Court Theatre. Irish Free State established.

1924 First Labour government. *Saint Joan* produced at the New Theatre. Death of Shaw's old friend, William Archer, and of the Italian actress whom he had so admired as a critic, Eleanora Duse.

1925 Shaw awarded Nobel Prize for Literature and uses it to endow English translations of Swedish literature, a start being made with the plays of Strindberg.

1926 General Strike in Britain.

1927 The Shaws move to Whitehall Court when Adelphi Terrace is demolished. Ellen Terry dies. *The Intelligent Woman's Guide to Capitalism and Socialism* published.

1929 Sir Barry Jackson, founder of the Birmingham Repertory Theatre, begins his mid-summer series of Malvern Festivals. *The Apple Cart* produced there. Second Labour government.

1930 World slump in trade begins. Huge losses in U.S.A. and much unemployment in many countries.

1931 Shaw visits Moscow. Politely welcomed by Stalin, but denounced as a conservative exponent of stale ideas in the Communist press. None the less he returns with high praise for the Soviet régime. Economic and political crisis in Britain. National government established. Labour, Liberal, and Conservative leaders form a Coalition Ministry, with Ramsay MacDonald remaining as Prime Minister but rejected by the majority of the Labour party, who oppose the Coalition.

1932 *Too True To Be Good* produced at Malvern and later at the New Theatre in London. In December the Shaws start on a world cruise. Hitler now leads biggest single party in Germany.

1933 Shaw in New York for one day in April. Delivers a serious lecture on *The Political Madhouse in America and Nearer Home*. Disappoints his audience and the Press who are expecting amusing Shavian entertainment. *On the Rocks* produced at Malvern and the Winter Garden Theatre in London. The fumbling of the National government together with his admiration of Russian Communism makes Shaw increasingly contemptuous of parliamentary democracy.

1934   All power now in the hands of the Nazi party in Germany. Two of Shaw's short plays, *The Village Wooing* and *The Six of Calais* produced.

1935   Shaw meets Gabriel Pascal and agrees on some filming of his work. *The Simpleton of the Unexpected Isles* produced at Malvern and the Prince's Theatre, London. General election in Britain puts Conservatives in power with Baldwin as Prime Minister.

1936   Death of King George V. Abdication of King Edward VIII who becomes Duke of Windsor. Shaw writes *The King, the Constitution, and the Lady*. *The Millionairess* produced at Bexhill. The chief part is subsequently played in London by Dame Edith Evans and Katharine Hepburn.

1937   Berlin-Rome Axis agreed between Hitler and Mussolini. Neville Chamberlain succeeds Baldwin as Prime Minister.

CANDIDA, *Globe, 1937*

1938   *Geneva* produced at Malvern and the Saville Theatre in London. Hitler and Neville Chamberlain sign the Munich Pact. Shaw threatened with pernicious anaemia but cured by liver injections.

1939   Hitler invades Czechoslovakia. *In Good King Charles's Golden Days* produced at Malvern and at the New Theatre in London in the following year. Outbreak of Second World War.

1940   Germans overrun France. Winston Churchill becomes Prime Minister.

1943   Death of Mrs Shaw after painful and crippling illness.

1944   Shaw publishes *Everybody's Political What's What*. 'D-Day' and invasion of Hitler's Europe.

1945   The age of atomic warfare arrives. End of war against Germany and Japan. Sweeping Labour victory at general election. Clement Attlee Prime Minister.

1946   Shaw's ninetieth birthday. He is able to broadcast and is made Freeman of Dublin and St Pancras. Death of Granville-Barker. Death of H. G. Wells.

1948   National Health Service begins.

1949   *Buoyant Billions* produced at Prince's Theatre, London. *Sixteen Self-Sketches* published.

1950   Shaw falls while pruning trees in his garden and taken to hospital in Luton. Desires to return home to Ayot St Lawrence. Dies there on November 2nd. His ashes with those of his wife scattered in the garden. In his will he had said, 'I prefer the garden to the cloister.'

BOOK LIST

Shaw maintained that a writer's life is in his work and that details of his comings and goings are tedious. In his own words, 'I have had no heroic adventures. Things have not happened to me; on the contrary, it is I who have happened to them; and all my happenings have taken the form of books and plays. Read them or spectate them and you have my whole story.'

While refusing to be voluminously autobiographical Shaw did, however, publish in 1949, a year before his death and at the age of ninety-three, a short book called *Sixteen Self-Sketches*. This contains a collection of spirited memories of his family, boyhood, and early life. There are also typically Shavian replies to correspondents who had asked him questions about his career and his opinions.

His principal and most substantial British biographers have been St John Ervine and Hesketh Pearson. Their books profited by the authors' friendship, conversations, and correspondence with Shaw. The fullest in scope is Mr Ervine's book, *Bernard Shaw, His Life, Work, and Friends*. This is particularly valuable for its account of Shaw's early work among Socialists and heretics of very different kinds and of the devoted service as well as leadership which he gave to the Fabian Society. There is candid criticism as well as warm appreciation of the plays, philosophy, and the man himself.

For the early Irish background *Lady Gregory* by Elizabeth Coxhead is very useful. The social background of Ireland and its Ascendancy class and Shaw's marriage to Charlotte Payne-Townshend are well described in *Mrs G.B.S.* by Janet Dunbar.

Shaw's theatrical criticisms (1895–98) were edited by James Huneker as *Dramatic Opinions and Essays* in two volumes in New York. Later they appeared in three volumes in the British Standard Edition, called *Our Theatres in the Nineties*. Important books on the theatrical life of the period are Laurence Irving's excellent study of his grandfather, *Henry Irving*, Ellen Terry's *Memoirs*, edited by Edith

Craig and Christopher St John, *About Theatres,* two volumes of Max Beerbohm's collected criticisms, and *William Poel* by Robert Speaight. The *Theatrical Companion to Shaw* by Raymond Mander and Joe Mitchenson gives an accurate pictorial record of the first performances of the plays.

Shaw's letters to and from Ellen Terry were edited by Christopher St John with a preface by G.B.S., Shaw's letters to Granville-Barker have been edited by C. B. Purdom and the correspondence with Mrs Patrick Campbell by Alan Dent. A comprehensive edition of Shaw's letters in several volumes is in preparation and will be published by the Bodley Head.

Shaw wrote and spoke much about the theatre in various journals and on various platforms. These pieces have been collected by E. J. West under the title of *Shaw on Theatre.* Edwin Wilson did a parallel service by collecting from *Dramatic Opinions* and other sources, and publishing with the title *Shaw on Shakespeare* what G.B.S. wrote about the Bard and the bardolators.

A choice of Shaw's political opinions was made by Dan Lawrence and called *Bernard Shaw, Platform and Pulpit.*

A gathering of local opinion among his neighbours at Ayot St Lawrence in Hertfordshire where Shaw had his country house was made after his death by Alan Chappelow and called *Shaw the Villager and Human Being.*

There are numerous critical studies of Shaw's life and work. G. K. Chesterton's *Bernard Shaw* was written in 1909 and therefore only takes Shaw to the age of fifty-three, but its liveliness in praise and opposition makes it still a pleasure to read. Maurice Colbourne's *The Real Bernard Shaw* gives a Shavian actor's view of the author of the plays and is also valuable for its chronology of Shaw's life and of productions of his plays at home and abroad.

Shaw's early work in fiction and pamphleteering was published by a variety of firms. The bulk of his work appeared under the imprint of Constable, whose Standard Edition keeps much of it in print.

The political life of the Left Wing during this period can be studied in *The History of the Fabian Society* by Edward R. Pease. Various aspects of Socialist theory can be found in the manifold sociological writings of H. G. Wells such as *A Modern Utopia*, in *The Acquisitive Society* by R. H. Tawney, and in *Guild Socialism* by G. D. H. Cole and William Mellor. The Distributist criticism of Socialism was tersely and vigorously stated by Hilaire Belloc in *The Servile State*. Throughout G. K. Chesterton's books there is constant defence of individualism against the State Socialism expounded by Shaw. G. M. Young's *Portrait of an Age* gives a richly informed and judicious picture of British society and its trends of thought and practice during the first half of Shaw's life.

INDEX